MONACO

David C. King

Marshall Cavendish
Benchmark
New York

PICTURE CREDITS
Cover photo: © Sergio Pitamitz/Danita Delimont
AFP/Getty Images: 44 • alt.TYPE/reuters: 34, 45, 54, 57, 59, 61, 62, 64, 112, 117, 121, 123 • Audrius Tomonis: 135 • Besstock: 16, 18, 19, 32, 58, 66, 67, 70, 71, 72, 73, 77, 78, 91, 97, 106, 107, 111, 129 • Bruce Yuan-Yue Bi/Lonely Planet Images: 87 • Carol Ann Wiley/ Lonely Planet Images: 46, 95 • Corbis: 6, 7, 8, 14, 21, 23, 30, 31, 38, 39, 40, 42, 43, 48, 56, 60, 65, 69, 79, 80, 82, 88, 89, 90, 101, 103, 105, 116, 118, 119, 120, 122, 124, 126, 128, 131 • Dallas Stribley/ Lonely Planet Images: 10, 13, 36, 76 • Eye Ubiquitous/Paul Thompson: 92 • Focus Team italy: 125 • Gilles Massot: 83 • James P. Blair/ National Geographic Image Collection: 50 • Jodi Cobb/ National Geographic Images Collection: 5, 20, 47, 51, 81, 83, 93, 94, 99, 100, 108 • Liba Taylor/ Hutchison: 74 Michael Coyne/Lonely Planet Images: 35 • Photolibrary: 1, 3, 4, 9, 11, 12, 15, 17, 25, 27, 28, 29, 33, 37, 41, 49, 53, 63, 68, 75, 85, 98, 104, 109, 110, 114, 115, 127 • STOCKFOOD/Brauner, M.: 130

PRECEDING PAGE
People at a café in front of Monaco's famous Monte-Carlo Casino.

Publisher (U.S.): Michelle Bisson
Editors: Christine Florie, Stephanie Pee
Copyreader: Tara Koellhoffer
Designers: Rachel Chen, Bernard Go Kwang Meng
Cover picture researcher: Connie Gardner
Picture researchers: Thomas Khoo, Joshua Ang

Marshall Cavendish Benchmark
99 White Plains Road
Tarrytown, NY 10591
www.marshallcavendish.us

© Times Media Private Limited 1997
© Marshall Cavendish International (Asia) Private Limited 2008
All rights reserved. First edition 1997. Second edition 2008.
® "Cultures of the World" is a registered trademark of Times Publishing Limited.

Originated and designed by Times Media Private Limited
An imprint of Marshall Cavendish International (Asia) Private Limited
A member of Times Publishing Limited

All Internet addresses were correct and accurate at the time of printing.

Library of Congress Cataloging-in-Publication Data
King, David, C.
  Monaco / David C. King
    p. cm. — (Cultures of the world)
  Summary: "Provides comprehensive information on the geography, history, governmental structure, economy, cultural diversity, peoples, religion, and culture of Monaco"—Provided by publisher.
  Includes bibliographical references and index.
  ISBN-13: 978-0-7614-2567-0
1. Monaco—Juvenile literature. I. Title. II. Series

  DC945.K54 2008
  944.9'49—dc22   2006030238

Printed in China
7 6 5 4 3 2 1

CONTENTS

Boats anchored at the Monaco harbor.

A guard on duty at the Monaco Palace.

INTRODUCTION

THE LUXURY TRAIN THAT BRINGS visitors to Monaco is known as the train to paradise. Many people think of this tiny country as a fairy-tale land, a paradise for the wealthy and famous. A cliff-top castle looks down on the scene of the 1956 "wedding of the century" between a beautiful Hollywood movie star and the ruling prince. The world's second-smallest country (only Vatican City is smaller) also boasts Monte-Carlo, the world's most famous gambling casino. Monaco features the Grand Prix race, in which brightly colored race cars roar around the narrow, winding streets at an average top speed of 88 miles (142 km) per hour.

Monaco is more than the glitter and excitement of the world's most luxurious resort. It is also a beautiful city-state of steep hills, outstanding architecture, unusual public gardens, and a thriving economy. The people do face 21st-century issues that are common in much larger countries, including environmental dangers and political issues such as building a democracy in the world's oldest ruling monarchy. Monaco is an intriguing country, with an unusual history and many surprises.

GEOGRAPHY

THE PRINCIPALITY OF MONACO IS PERCHED on the Mediterranean coast, close to the Italian border, and is surrounded on three sides by France's Provence-Alpes-Côte d'Azure region. This area is better known as the Riviera. The rocky foothills of the Alps rise abruptly from the sparkling blue of the Mediterranean Sea. Monaco's highest point, Mont Agel, is a rocky promontory, or headland, that rises 460 feet (140 m) above the sea.

With an area of just three-quarters of a square mile (1.9 square km), Monaco is about half the size of New York's Central Park. Its population of more than 32,000 would not quite fill half of New York's Yankee Stadium. Because its area is so small, however, the number of people who live in the country makes Monaco the most densely populated nation in the world.

Left: **The royal palace.**

Opposite: **The sparkling blue waters of Côte d'Azur.**

The mild, sunny Mediterranean climate is only one of Monaco's great appeals. The average temperature year-round is 61°F (16°C) with more than 300 days of sunshine. The temperature ranges from an average of 54°F (10°C) in January to 82°F (28°C) in August.

AREAS

Although Monaco covers an area of less than one square mile, it is divided into five sections, or areas. They are Monaco-Ville, La Condamine, Monte-Carlo, Fontvieille, and Moneghetti.

The oldest part of the city-state is Monaco-Ville, situated on the Rock of Monaco. The Rock is a steep-sided finger of land that is flat

Opposite: **Apartments lining the streets of Monaco-Ville.**

Below: **Monaco-Ville is situated on the Rock of Monaco.**

on top and extends 2,600 feet (792 m) into the Mediterranean Sea. From almost any point on this promontory, there are breathtaking views of the sea and the entire Principality of Monaco.

A very steep red-brick pedestrian pathway called Rampe Major, built in the 1500s, connects the port area to the palace on top of the Rock of Monaco. The maze of narrow, twisting streets and covered walkways is crowded with villas, apartment buildings, and the shops of Old Town. This picturesque area, with modern buildings challenging ancient structures that were built hundreds of years ago, also contains public gardens, several museums, and the majestic Cathedral of Monaco.

La Condamine is the area around Monaco's port. It can be reached from the top of the Rock by the Rampe Major or by the most unusual feature of Monaco's transportation system: a number of escalators and elevators (called lifts) that connect the steepest streets. La Condamine is a shopping and commercial center with a promenade along the harbor, where visitors can gaze at the dazzling array of cruise ships and luxury yachts.

The original Port of Monaco is located at La Condamine. To the west of the Port of Monaco is a smaller and newer harbor, the Port of Fontvieille. Between 1966 and 1973

an ambitious landfill project reclaimed 74 acres (22 ha) of land from the sea, pushing the southernmost region of Monaco into the Mediterranean and forming a new harbor between Fontvieille and Monaco proper.

Fontvieille quickly became the home of Monaco's new light industries. These businesses primarily include cosmetics and electronics companies, as well as other nonpolluting firms. This area has also

THE WORLD'S LARGEST FLOATING DIKE

The original Port of Monaco, also called Port Hercule (*left*), was built between 1901 and 1926. Its size was adequate for most of the 20th century. With the rapidly expanding number—and size—of both cruise ships and private yachts, Prince Rainier III, the ruler of Monaco for more than 50 years, felt it was essential to expand the port's capacity. The solution was to construct an enormous floating dike. The 163,000-ton (147,871-metric-ton) hulk took 700 workers in Spain nearly three years to construct. The dike is 92 feet (28 m) wide and 1,154 feet (352 m) long. In August 2002 it was towed to Monaco, where it has doubled Monaco's port capacity, making the Port of Monaco one of the world's leading cruise-ship harbors.

become known as Monaco's "collector's corner" because a number of museums are located here. In addition, Fontvieille has a small pond and a spectacular rose garden. More than 4,000 rose bushes form Princess Grace's Rose Garden, which was planted in honor of one of Monaco's most beloved princesses, the late Princess Grace, who married Prince Rainier III in 1984. The rose garden adjoins other exotic gardens in Parc Fontvieille, including a coastal path called Chemin des Sculptures (Sculpture Road), which is lined with contemporary sculptures.

The heights of Monte-Carlo are probably the most famous of Monaco's areas. In fact, many outsiders assume that the area of Monte-Carlo is Monaco. The most magical part of the region is the Place du Casino

The arch of flowers at the Chemin des Sculptures.

The Monte Carlo Casino is world renowned and attracts the rich and famous to the principality.

and the Square Beaumarchais. The great gambling casino and some of Europe's most elegant hotels and restaurants have made this a gathering place for royalty and millionaires for more than a century. In the 21st century, Monte-Carlo has drawn the most famous names in sports and entertainment. There are few places in the world that can match the extravagant lifestyle that Monte-Carlo displays.

Many of the region's 19th-century villas are being replaced by high-rise apartments; so much so that people jokingly call Monte-Carlo "New York on the Mediterranean" because of its skyline of tall buildings. In spite of the intrusion of modern high-rise buildings, Monte-Carlo retains a spectacular display of architectural styles, some dating back to the 14th and 15th centuries. Another beautiful feature of this region is the terracing of the steep hills. There are

also numerous gardens that surround the casino with bright colors and greenery.

To the east of Monte-Carlo is Larvotto, Monaco's only beach area, with both public and private sections. In the private section, bathers can rent cushioned sun-lounges and colorful parasols. The last major construction project of Prince Rainier III was the Grimaldi Forum Monaco, which was completed in 2000. The forum is used as a conference center and also houses art exhibits, cultural center ballets, operas, and dance performances.

Monaco's fifth area is Moneghetti, a unique area on the western edge of the country that features an exotic garden of tropical and subtropical plants. The Mediterranean climate allows plants to survive much farther north than in other parts of Europe. The garden is aptly

Larvotto Beach is often crowded with people looking to soak up some of Monaco's plentiful sunshine.

named Jardin Exotique (Exotic Garden). It was constructed by terracing the sheer cliffs, a task that took 20 years. The terraced gardens are connected by footbridges, and secluded spots are formed by dense foliage. Caring for the gardens requires specialists to be suspended in parachute harnesses.

At the foot of the Exotic Garden cliff is a series of amazing caves, called Grottes de l'Observatoire (Observatory Caves). Visitors climb down 279 steps (most of which are slippery with moisture) inside the hillside, where they enter a series of caves naturally decorated with countless stalagmites and stalactites. This is the only cave system in Europe where the temperature becomes warmer as one descends. Some caves feature

A gardener in a parachute harness descending the wall of Jardin Exotique in order to tend to its plants.

ice-blue pools and natural sculptures. The largest cave, called La Grande Salle (The Great Room) resembles a cathedral, complete with rock pillars and a rock sculpture shaped like a baptismal font. As in all the caves, there is an eerie silence except for the gentle sound of dripping water.

The most remarkable features of the caves are some prehistoric rock drawings that are among the oldest in the world. Scientists estimate that the "rock scratches" may have been made one million years ago. The scenes depict prehistoric animals, including early reindeer. The cave complex is also home to the Museum of Prehistoric Anthropology, with displays of human evolution, as well as the bones of reindeer, mammoths, and hippopotami.

Beautiful stalagmites and stalactites can be found in the Grotte de l'Observatorie.

Le Jardin Exotique is home to thousands of exotic plants and is tended to by diligent gardeners everyday.

A LAND OF SPECTACULAR GARDENS

Monaco has very little in the way of natural flora and fauna. In terms of wildlife, Monaco has only 22 species of amphibians, birds, mammals, and reptiles, according to the World Conservation Monitoring Center.

Monaco's plant life is also difficult to describe because there are virtually no plants growing wild. There are no fields and no forests. Instead, the people of Monaco and the government have created some of the most spectacular gardens in Europe.

Le Jardin Exotique, for example, on the steep cliff face near the caves, was started in 1933 with several thousand succulents and cacti planted in crevices and ledges within the sheer rock wall. Since then, roughly 2,000 more exotic plants have been added. Winding paths and flimsy-looking footbridges connect different sections; some bridges hang precariously

above African *candelabra* cacti, which grow to heights of more than 30 feet (9 m). Another towering cactus is the Moroccan euphorbia, which reaches 50 feet (15 m). A favorite among visitors is the Mexican echino cactus, which looks like a guinea pig with sharp spikes and is popularly known as a "mother-in-law's pillow." For those who dare to look up while traversing the bridges, the garden offers spectacular views of the harbor, the Mediterranean, and part of the French Riviera.

Another popular garden is the Jardin Japonais (Japanese Garden). It was built to offer a corner of quiet and peace, and was blessed by a Shinto priest. Visitors are encouraged to use the Zen garden for meditation and contemplation.

Two beautiful gardens grace the heights of Monte-Carlo. The Jardins du Casino (Casino Gardens) surround the casino with bright splashes of color, and additional interest is provided by changing art exhibits along the center pathway.

Many locals and tourists visit the tranquil and serene Japanese Garden for its beauty and peace.

Nearby, just outside the cathedral, is the exotic Jardins Saint Martin (Saint Martin Gardens). Aleppo pines and yellow agaves cover terraces that wind around the Rock of Monaco. Scattered through the greenery are medieval fortifications and turrets built in the 1700s. As with all of Monaco's gardens, these are perfectly tended by teams of gardeners dressed in uniform.

VIEWING WILDLIFE

Monaco also has some intriguing opportunities for viewing wildlife. The Zoological Terraces, for example, showcase animals that have been brought in from tropical regions. Many of the animals are only temporary residents, staying long enough to become accustomed to life in captivity before being sent to European zoos. At any one time,

visitors might see a pair of young rhinos, a black panther, and an albino, or white tiger.

The most famous wildlife-viewing area is the Musée Océanographique (Oceanographic Museum). It was built by Prince Albert I in 1910 as a "temple of the sea." The aquarium is regarded as one of the world's most outstanding aquariums, and its 90 tanks are used for research as well as to display marine life. The famous marine explorer Jacques-Yves Cousteau was director of the museum for 30 years, until 1988.

The highlight of the museum is a 24.5-foot-long (7.5-m-long) live coral reef transplanted from tropical waters, with brightly colored tropical fish on one side and ocean predators on the other, including cat sharks and white-and-black-tipped reef sharks. The sharks ominously circle a wrecked boat that is home to blue and yellow sturgeon. The sea creatures consume 8,800 pounds (4,000 kg) of food every day.

A black tip reef shark on display in one of the Oceanographic Museum's aquariums.

HISTORY

THE HISTORY OF MONACO IS STEEPED in mystery and intrigue. Monaco's history before A.D. 1000 is extremely sketchy and is shrouded in mystery because records and any evidence of the past have been buried under millions of tons of concrete. There is hardly a square foot of this tiny principality that has not been paved or built on.

One reason for the intrigue has been that Monaco exists in the shadow of two gigantic neighbors: France and Italy. France has taken control of Monaco on several occasions, and in the 21st century it continues to be responsible for the defense of Monaco's independence and sovereignty.

Monaco's relations with Italy have been unusual because there was no unified nation of Italy until the mid-19th century. For a thousand

Opposite: **The Monaco Cathedral.**

Below: **Petroglyphs like these dating from the Bronze Age provide scientists and researchers with evidence and information on activities of people during that time.**

years before unification the peninsula was divided into a number of competing city-states, including Genoa, Florence, Venice, and the Vatican. The struggles among these powers have frequently involved Monaco, which was sometimes taken over by Genoa. The Grimaldi family, which has ruled Monaco for many centuries, are actually descendents of Genovese statesmen and were also one of Genoa's most powerful ruling families.

EARLY HISTORY

The caves of Monaco and the coastal area around it provide evidence of the presence of early humans dating to about 400,000 years ago. Stone Age hunters scratched pictures on the walls of a cave deep inside the Rock of Monaco. These drawings, which are among the oldest cave art in the world, are protected in the Grottes de l'Observatoire, Monaco's famous Cave Observatory.

The coastal region around Monaco has provided evidence of Neanderthal hunters, who roamed the Mediterranean coast from about 90,000 B.C. to 40,000 B.C. The first modern humans arrived around 30,000 B.C. They lived by hunting and gathering wild foods, then began growing crops around 6000 B.C. The caves display remarkably modern-looking cave art (or petroglyphs) of bison, seals, deer, and other animals. One of the greatest collections of Bronze Age petroglyphs is in the "Valley of Wonders," located a few miles from the France-Italy border. More than 36,000 cave paintings depict human figures as well as animals. The art was created between 1800 B.C. and 1500 B.C.

By about 1000 B.C. Monaco was part of a lively Mediterranean sea trade that involved civilizations from places such as Phoenicia and Greece in the east and Rome and Carthage in the west. The ancient

Greeks established a number of coastal trading posts. One was probably set up at Monaco around 600 B.C.

Historians believe that the name Monaco is derived from the name of the Greek colony of Monoikos. Monoikos was probably located in the area that became Monaco, which included land between the Rock of Monaco and the border of Italy. This larger Monaco, which existed until 1848, was about nine times larger than the present principality. The Greeks introduced grapes and olives to this area, which was already famous for its lemon orchards.

Rome moved into the area about 120 B.C. During the height of the Roman Empire, roads and aqueducts were built along the coast from Italy to Spain. The greater Monaco flourished under Roman rule, providing Rome with olive oil, wine, and lemons. After the fall of Rome in the 5th century, various Germanic tribes invaded the area. Little is known of Monaco's history over the next 500 years. Gradually the region came under the influence of Genoa, one of the ambitious Italian city-states.

The area of Roquebrune, north of present day Monaco, was once part of greater Monaco.

Opposite: **A statue in honor of François Grimaldi who disguised himself as a monk to gain access into the fortress of Monaco.**

POWER STRUGGLES

Modern Monaco and its ruling family emerged from the political maneuverings and wars of Renaissance Italy. For several hundred years, the city-state of Genoa was one of the most powerful in Italy, vying for wealth and influence with Naples, Venice, and the Vatican. The Grimaldi family provided many of Genoa's political, religious, and military leaders.

One of the Grimaldi family's rivals for power in Genoa, the Ghibellines, was in control of the enlarged Monaco. In 1297 François Grimaldi hatched a plot to seize control of Monaco and then use it as a base of operations against the Ghibellines in Genoa itself.

MURDER AND INTRIGUE

The city-states and monarchs of southern Europe were often involved in all sorts of political maneuvering and intrigue. From about A.D. 1100 to the middle of the 19th century, Monaco was often caught up in such events, especially since members of the Grimaldi family were eager to gain or hold power.

In the early 1500s, for example, after a quarrel with the French king, the Grimaldis turned to Spain for protection. However, there was political bickering within the family and in 1505 Prince Jean II was murdered by his brother, Lucien. A few years later Lucien was murdered by another relative. Later in the early 1600s Monaco was rocked by a revolt, and Prince Honore I was drowned by some of his subjects. It was not until the mid-1800s that France agreed to guarantee Monaco's independence in exchange for its recognition of Menton and Roquebrune as French territory.

With a small band of soldiers, Grimaldi went to the Ghibelline fortress on the Rock of Monaco. With his men hidden in a garden, he disguised himself as a monk and knocked on the door in the fortress gate. When two soldiers answered, Grimaldi asked for a night's lodging. As soon as the soldiers let him in he drew a dagger from his robe and murdered them. Grimaldi and his men quickly gained control of the fortress and all of Monaco. Although there have been some gaps in their control, the Grimaldis have been Monaco's ruling family since François' brazen act.

Over the next century, the Grimaldis lost and regained control of Monaco several times as the struggle for power among Italy's states continued. Two Grimaldi brothers gained control in 1395, for example, but promptly lost it to France. Then, in 1419, another Grimaldi took final possession of Monaco, although the family did not start to use the title "prince" until 1659. Except for the few times they lost sovereignty, therefore, the Grimaldis can be considered Europe's oldest ruling family.

Because Monaco shares most of its borders with France, the Grimaldi princes have found it useful to maintain friendly relations with the

French. However, for a little more than a century, from 1524 to 1641, Monaco was under the protection of Spain. Subsequently, in 1793, during the French Revolution, Monaco was annexed to France. The turbulence of the Italian city-states was replaced by the turbulence of the French Revolution and the Napoleonic wars that raged across Europe and the high seas from the 1790s to 1814.

At the Congress of Vienna, a meeting of all the great powers of Europe, the Grimaldis were returned to power and Monaco was placed under the protection of Sardinia. The Grimaldi family spent several years in prison during the upheaval of the French Revolution. When they were released they had to sell most of their possessions in order to survive. In addition the palace had been used as a warehouse and needed major repairs.

Even though the Grimaldis were once again the ruling family of Monaco, their problems were far from over. In 1848 the territories of Menton and Roquebrune revolted against Monaco's high taxes and demanded their independence. These two areas had been part of the enlarged Monaco for hundreds of years, and their olives, oranges, and lemons had been Monaco's main source of income. When they gained independence Monaco suddenly lost more than 90 percent of its land area and quickly became the poorest country in Europe. In 1861 Monaco signed a new treaty with France in which France again recognized Monaco's independence and Monaco officially accepted the loss of Menton and Roquebrune. In 1865 a financial treaty was signed that involved customs duties and promised future cooperation between the two countries.

MODERN MONACO

In 1863 Monaco's Prince Charles III built the first part of the gambling casino, naming it Monte-Carlo (Mount Charles) in 1866. He modeled it after a famous gambling resort in Baden-Baden, Germany, which drew dazzling crowds of monarchs, dukes and duchesses, and other royalty, as well as Europe's wealthiest men and women. Prince Charles hoped that Monte-Carlo would be a similar source of riches. He hired outstanding architects and designers to produce a remarkably ornate and rich style, with stained-glass skylights and windows, as well as enormous bronze lamps. Other luxurious buildings, such as the Hôtel de Paris and the Café de Paris provided the wealthy and titled Europeans with reasons to plan excursions and vacations to Monte-Carlo.

The casino provided the income source that Monaco desperately needed. Within five years Prince Charles was able to do away with

The residence of the royal family—The Palace of the Prince—was originally built as a fortress in 1191.

income taxes. The prince had been worried about the possible negative effects of gambling, so, from the beginning, citizens of Monaco were forbidden to gamble in the casino.

With its economic base secure for the time being, the Grimaldi rulers could concentrate on other ways to modernize their little city-state. One of the most popular princes was Albert I (1848–1922). In 1911 he gave Monaco a constitution that provided for limited participation in the government through an elected National Council. The National Council was granted almost no power beyond advising, but it was hailed as a step toward democracy.

Another important step taken by Prince Albert I was arranging another treaty with France in 1918, at the end of World War I (1914–18). The treaty provided that, in the event that a Grimaldi ruling

An artist's rendering of Monte-Carlo Casino in 1900.

prince died without leaving an heir, Monaco would become a self-ruling state under the French constitution.

Like the rest of Europe, Monaco enjoyed the fast-paced life of the Roaring Twenties. American and European movie stars and famous athletes joined the parade of rich and famous people who vacationed in Monaco. The harbor became increasingly crowded with luxury yachts, and famous artists like Pablo Picasso discovered the beauty of the beaches, with the sparkling Mediterranean and deep blue sky. In 1929 the first Grand Prix auto race brought together brilliantly colored race cars that roared around the sharp turns and steep hills. The race quickly became one of Europe's premier sports events.

Monaco fell on hard times during the Great Depression of the 1930s. Because so much wealth was lost throughout Europe, revenues declined sharply at the casino and surrounding businesses.

Just as the world was beginning to recover from the Great Depression, Europe and the world were plunged into World War II (1939–45) because of the aggression of Nazi Germany, Fascist Italy, and militaristic Japan. The war years formed a dark chapter in Monaco's story. First, Prince Louis II (1870-49) declared that Monaco would remain neutral, but he actively supported the Vichy government, a regime set up in the southern half of France by Nazi Germany.

Prince Albert I was a farsighted, popular ruler who implemented many positive changes for his people.

The pro-Nazi stance of Louis II created a deep rift between Louis and his grandson, Rainier III (1923–2005). Rainier spent the war years fighting with the Free French against Nazi Germany. Prince Louis II, by contrast, allowed the Nazis to "launder" money that they had pillaged from the conquered nations of Europe by setting up banks in Monaco. Monaco's annual revenues increased from 3 million francs to 80 million. Louis II also allowed the Gestapo (the Nazi secret police) to set up their headquarters in the Hôtel de Paris. Prince Rainier III was furious over reports that Jewish refugees, who were seeking to escape Nazi concentration camps, had mysteriously "disappeared" from Monaco's hotels. He blamed his grandfather's minister of state, Émile Roblot, for these actions and demanded his removal, but Louis refused. Supporters

Prince Rainier III in uniform during World War II.

of Prince Louis insisted that he was at the mercy of Nazi power and had no choice but to give in to German demands.

"THE BUILDER PRINCE"

Prince Rainier III succeeded his grandfather as the ruler of Monaco in 1949 and dominated the country's affairs for the next 56 years. He knew that the country needed a diversified economy. Monte-Carlo

A park leading up to Hôtel de Paris where the Gestapo were allowed to set up their headquarters during World War II.

**Prince Rainier III and
Princess Grace.**

could not provide enough revenue, especially after gambling casinos were opened in France and other countries. Through advertising and promotional campaigns, he transformed Monaco into a mecca for tourists, adding on to its luxurious facilities. Once a winter spa centered on gambling at Monte-Carlo, Monaco now became a summer vacationland as well, with an ambitious buildup of beach and harbor facilities.

Other building projects enabled Rainier to increase Monaco's boundaries. The great floating dike doubled the port facilities, and the landfill at Fontvieille made room for the construction of nonpolluting light industries.

In 1955 Hollywood film star Grace Kelly arrived in Monaco to shoot a film. She was presented to the prince for a photo shoot at the Monégasque palace. A whirlwind romance led to the "wedding of the century" one year later. The event captured the romantic imagination of people everywhere.

Princess Grace never made another Hollywood film. Instead, she devoted herself to her royal duties. The beauty and dignity of the princess, and the fairy-tale wedding, added luster to Monaco's appeal as a tourist center and destination. Throughout the next two decades, the yacht harbor, beaches, and hotels witnessed a steady procession of the rich and famous from around the world. The prince continued his building projects, leading Princess Grace to complain, jokingly, that people could not sunbathe on the beaches after 3:00 P.M. because of the shadow cast by Rainier's high-rise apartment buildings.

In 1982 Princess Grace died in an automobile accident on one of Monaco's notoriously steep hairpin turns. She was reported as having suffered from a stroke while driving. The tragedy was a blow to the glamorous, fairy-tale atmosphere of the principality. In the years that followed the royal image became seriously tarnished by personal scandals involving the royal couple's three children—Caroline, Albert, and Stephanie.

Early in 2000 Prince Rainier finished his last ambitious construction project: the Grimaldi Forum Monaco, a huge glass structure between Monte Carlo and the sea. The building is used for occasional art

The Grimaldi Forum Monaco is used for art exhibitions and conventions.

exhibitions in addition to business conferences. His hopes for an imaginative project to build out farther into the Mediterranean by making use of Monaco's territorial waters had to be put on hold when the 80-year-old prince's health began to fail. In March 2005 Prince Albert, marquis of Baux, took over the royal duties because his father was too ill to carry them out.

Prince Rainier died on April 6, 2005, and his son succeeded him as Prince Albert II of Monaco. On July 12, 2005, the formal accession took place. It included a solemn Mass at the cathedral where his father had been buried three months earlier.

The Grimaldi family at the funeral of Prince Rainier III.

ROYAL TRAPPINGS

The official residence of the prince, the Palais Princier, was redesigned by Princess Grace, changing the pale yellow exterior walls to salmon pink. When the prince's standard is raised, the prince is at home and the 235-room palace is closed to visitors. Each day, however, hundreds of visitors come to observe the changing of the guard. At 11:55 P.M. the 98 guards, called the Carabiniers du Prince (the prince's guards), perform the precise and colorful ceremony. (None of the guards is a citizen of Monaco—a precaution designed to prevent palace revolts.) In summer the carabiniers are dressed in brilliant white; in winter they wear blue with red stripes.

A tour of the Grand State apartments includes the Musée des Souvenirs Napoléoniens et Archives Historiques du Palais (Museum of Napoleonic Souvenirs and the Palace's Historic Archive) in the palace's southern wing. This includes fascinating displays of medals, coins, weapons, and strangely, a pair of Napoleon's socks.

GOVERNMENT

MONACO'S GOVERNMENT IS UNIQUE among the world's 200 nations. Apart from the Vatican, Monaco is the smallest country in the world. It is also the oldest continuously ruling monarchy in history. Another unusual feature of the government is that, until recently, the prince ruled with absolute authority, but the people have not appeared to feel oppressed because of the benevolent nature of the government. Today Monaco is a constitutional monarchy that places some limits on royal authority.

In spite of the principality's lack of size and power, the government functions with great pageantry. The changing of the guard at the prince's palace, for example, is carried out with pomp and precision that is not unlike the changing of the guard at England's Buckingham Palace. Every day large crowds gather outside the palace gates for the 11:55 A.M. ceremony. The 98 members of the Carabiniers du Prince (the prince's

Left: **The changing of the guards ceremony takes place at the prince's palace.**

Opposite: **The flag of Monaco displayed proudly in front of Monaco's iconic Monte-Carlo casino.**

guards) put on an elaborate display of precision marching, with the sun glistening off their brilliant white summer uniforms and helmets. (Winter uniforms are deep blue with a red stripe.)

Other affairs of state have also involved colorful ceremonies. The 1956 marriage of Prince Rainier III and Hollywood film star Grace Kelly was memorable for its elaborate displays, including the bride's arrival in a harbor filled with yachts and boats, while a seaplane scattered red and white carnations across the water. The sky was filled with fireworks, while Monégasque and American flags parachuted down. Hundreds of guests filled the cathedral for the ceremony, while thousands more celebrated in the streets.

The fairy-tale wedding of American film star Grace Kelly and Prince Rainier III of Monaco captured the romantic imagination of many around the world.

In 1997 Monaco celebrated 700 years of the Grimaldi dynasty. Once again, there were great displays of fireworks and noisy street celebrations, but the 1956 wedding continues to stand out as the principality's fairy-tale moment.

The present-day area of Menton. The loss of the region dealt a severe blow to the economy of Monaco.

MONACO AND FRANCE

France looms over Monaco as a gigantic force. In the event of a power struggle, French strength would easily swallow up the tiny city-state. Over the centuries, the Grimaldi princes have worked out agreements with their huge neighbor that have allowed Monaco to retain its independence. A treaty signed in 1861, for example, confirmed the principality's independence in exchange for accepting the loss of the regions of Menton and Roquebrune, which had rebelled in 1848 and were annexed by France.

There have been several other treaties to clarify relations. Under the terms of a treaty signed in 1918, if a royal prince dies without an heir, Monaco will become an independent city-state under French protection.

Late in the 20th century, Monaco's insistence on having no income tax led to a serious dispute with France. Hundreds of wealthy French families established residences in Monaco so as to take advantage of the tax-free status. Several agreements were tried, but people always found loopholes. When Prince Rainier III refused to impose taxes in 1962, President Charles de Gaulle of France responded by closing all the borders into Monaco. De Gaulle's action forced Prince Rainier to

French President Charles de Gaulle meeting crowds of French people in 1961.

renegotiate and sign a new treaty with France in 1963. French citizens with less than five years' residence in Monaco would now be taxed at French rates. In addition, graduated taxes were imposed on Monégasque companies that conducted more than 25 percent of their business outside the principality.

Although France has a good deal of influence over Monaco, the principality continues to function as an independent nation. Monaco became a member of the United Nations in 1993 and has been active in several international bodies, including the European Organization for Security and Cooperation. The principality also has consulates in many European countries, as well as in the United States and Canada.

Monaco also goes its own way in financial matters. It did not become a member of the European Union, for example, instead preferring to

The steps leading up to private bank, Barclays, in Monaco. Monaco's banking and financial policies have attracted many foreign investors, boosting the country's economy.

maintain a customs union with France. This enables Monaco to use France's currency, which now happens to be the euro. Monaco even has the right to mint euro coins, with Monégasque designs on one side.

The principality is determined to protect its liberal tax system and its confidentiality banking rules that attract many foreign investors. In 2000 a French government report accused Monaco of lax policies regarding banking practices and taxes. The Monégasque government quickly investigated the claim and issued reports showing that nearly all the charges were inaccurate.

Opposite: **Prince Albert II presenting the Grimaldi reign logo in celebration of 700 years of rule.**

Below: **Monaco's currency is now the Euro.**

THE RULE OF THE GRIMALDIS

Since the late 13th century, every prince of Monaco has been a member of the Grimaldi family. No other family in history has dominated a government for so long.

The family first became powerful in Genoa, one of several city-states that vied for power in Italy until the nation was finally unified in the 1860s. The Grimaldis and another family dominated Genoa's Guelph Party in ongoing struggles with the Ghibelline Party. The conflict often spilled over into surrounding areas, and Monaco was caught in the middle. There were also times when the power struggles involved nearly all of Europe, including Spain and France. From time to time the people of Monaco found themselves living under the protection of Spain, France, or even the kingdom of Sardinia in the early 1800s. Most of the time, however, the Grimaldis remained at the helm.

The dynasty almost came to an end in 1731, when Prince Antoine I died without leaving a male heir. His daughter took over and ruled as princess, keeping the family line intact.

Monaco was fortunate to have two far-sighted rulers in the 19th and early 20th centuries. Prince Charles III (1818–89) negotiated the treaty of 1861 that guaranteed Monaco's independence,

then built the fabled Monte-Carlo Casino to provide both the family and the principality with income to offset the loss of Menton and Roquebrune.

Prince Charles III was succeeded by Prince Albert I (1848–1922). Albert was known as the seafaring prince because of his many ocean voyages and his keen interest in marine biology. He founded the world-famous Oceanographic Museum (and another in Paris). He also provided Monaco with its first constitution in 1911, creating a limited democracy.

In the 20th century, the rule of Prince Louis II (1870–1949) was a less happy time. His pro-Nazi sympathies and policies divided the people and

On the Grimaldi coat of arms there are two monks upholding the shield, which represents François Grimaldi who disguised himself as a monk. The Grimaldi motto reads *Deo Juvante*, meaning "with God's help."

infuriated his grandson, Rainier. Prince Rainier III took the throne in 1949 and ruled for 56 years, by far the longest reign of any European prince.

THE GOVERNMENT STRUCTURE

The Grimaldis had no real check on their authority until 1911, when Prince Albert I agreed to Monaco's first constitution. The people—adult male citizens at least—were given a limited voice in the government through an elected National Council. The council could pass new laws, which then had to be approved by the prince. In 1959, in a dispute with the council, Prince Rainier III suspended parts of the constitution, dissolved the National Council and, in 1961, created a National Assembly made up of people whom he had appointed.

The crisis with France over the taxation issue forced Prince Rainier III to reconsider his actions. To satisfy French president de Gaulle as well as his own people, Prince Rainier III got rid of his National Assembly, restored the National Council, and granted a very liberal constitution.

The steps of the Palais de Justice (the law courts) in Monaco-ville.

The National Council originally consisted of 18 members, but this number has since been changed to 24. Sixteen members are elected by majority vote and eight others are elected on the basis of proportional representation—a formula based on the percentage of votes that each party received in the last election. Voting is by universal suffrage and the members' terms are for five years.

In the early 21st century, two main political parties were formed: the National and Democratic Union (UND) and the Union for Monaco (UPM), which now also includes the National Union for the Future of Monaco (UNAM). In the most recent elections held in February 2003, UNAM elected 21 members into the council and the UND elected three. The next election is scheduled for February 2008. The council shares legislative power with the prince. The monarch has the power to veto legislation.

The day-to-day functions of government are conducted by the minister of state. In the past, the minister had to be a French citizen. He or she was appointed by the prince from a list provided by the French government. That requirement, which gave France considerable influence over Monaco's government, has since been changed. The minister can now be a citizen of Monaco.

The judiciary system has been modeled on that of France since 1819. Trials are held before a panel of three judges, rather than a single judge and a jury. Two French judges form a Court of Appeals.

PRINCE RAINIER

Prince Rainier (1923–2005) was the 31st hereditary ruler of the principality. His original name was Rainier-Louis-Henri-Maxence-Bertrand de Grimaldi. He was the son of Prince Pierre, comte de Polignac, and Princess Charlotte de Monaco. Princess Charlotte was the daughter of Louis II, so Rainier received his Grimaldi name through her, not through his father.

Prince Rainier was sent to Switzerland and England for his education and then attended a university in France. During World War II (1939–45), he served with the French Army and after the war he attended the University of Paris. He began his reign in 1949, a month before his grandfather Louis II died.

Prince Rainier was an energetic and forceful ruler. His ambitious plans for the floating dike and for the landfill that created the Fontvieille section have doubled Monaco's port facilities and increased the principality's land area by nearly 25 percent.

The fairy-tale marriage of Prince Rainier and Grace Kelly added to the prince's popularity. Princess Grace devoted herself to her royal duties and to raising their three children—Caroline, Albert, and Stephanie. Her tragic death in 1982 took much of the luster off the prince's storybook reign. In addition, the escapades of his three grown children, which were often splashed across the pages of the tabloids, led many to feel that Rainier's rule was star-crossed, or cursed by bad luck. Rainier maintained his dignity and ruled efficiently until late 2004, a few months before his death in 2005. He was succeeded by his son Albert, who became Prince Albert II on April 6, 2005.

ECONOMY

IN THE 1860S TINY MONACO HAD the sad distinction of being the poorest country in Europe. When the regions of Menton and Roquebrune declared their independence in 1848, they reduced Monaco's land area by almost 95 percent and left Monaco with no arable land. These provinces were major food producers for Monaco. In addition, the products of those provinces, especially oranges, lemons, and olive oil, were the major sources of revenue for the state.

The loss of revenue and the need to import food plunged Monaco into poverty. Since those difficult years, the energy of the people and the creative planning of several monarchs have not only restored the principality, but also give it one of the world's highest standards of living.

Oppposite: **A woman sewing uniforms for the staff of the Monte-Carlo Hotel.**

Below: **The loss of vineyards and plantations like this caused Monaco to become one of the poorest countries in Europe.**

49

THE CASINO GAMBLE

Monaco's Prince Charles III took a big chance when he opened the first part of the casino in 1863. His only model was a summertime health spa and gambling casino in the German town of Baden-Baden. He thought that the same combination of health and gambling might attract wealthy Europeans who wanted to escape the northern winter. He also wanted the world to take notice of his principality. The prince was aware of the pitfalls of gambling, so he made it illegal for anyone in his family, or any citizen of Monaco, to gamble or even to enter the premises.

The Casino de Monte-Carlo was constructed in three stages. First was the Salon de l'Europe, with eight magnificent crystal chandeliers

The famous Monte Carlo casino is often considered to be the jewel of Monaco.

added in 1898. For the second phase, the prince hired Europe's leading architect, Charles Garnier, who had just completed the great Paris Opera. Garnier created an extravagant building with frescoes. The Salle Garnier was completed in 1878, the same year as the great entrance hall with its 28 marble columns. The third part, the Salle Médecin, was completed in 1910.

The opulent surroundings proved to be a great attraction in their own right, especially for the wealthiest people of Europe and America. Prince Charles III also added other luxury elements: Les Thermes Marins de Monte-Carlo, for example, was a fantastic spa, featuring special treatments such as shiatsu massages, a pool of heated seawater, and a skin treatment with diamond dust. In addition, Monte-Carlo offered some of Europe's most extravagant hotels and restaurants. The Hôtel

The extravagant and famous Louis XV restaurant in Hôtel de Paris.

de Paris includes a gold-decorated restaurant named Louis XV, which boasts of one of the world's largest wine cellar—250,000 bottles stored in a rock cave.

Ownership and management of the casino is in the hands of a corporation: the Société des Baines de Mer (Society of Sea Bathing; SBM). SBM continues to operate today, controlled by the government, and it is Monaco's major employer. The corporation owns and operates several of the most luxurious hotels and restaurants.

The combination of excellent facilities, a sun-filled Mediterranean climate, the beach and harbor facilities, and the lure of gambling provided Monaco with enormous potential as a year-round resort, and its success surpassed the prince's most optimistic dreams. By the 1880s and 1890s Monte-Carlo was the jewel of European resorts, drawing the wealthiest and most famous families from throughout Europe and the Americas.

The heyday of the Monte-Carlo complex continued through the 1920s. The "Roaring Twenties" brought new visitors and spenders. Famous movie stars, great sports figures, jazz musicians, and even American underworld figures were attracted to the Monte-Carlo. All they had to do was follow Monte-Carlo's rules of dress and conduct in order to enter the casino and the best hotels and restaurants. In 1929 the first Formula One Grand Prix automobile race was run—a prestigious event that continues to be a major attraction. Wealthy spectators watch the event and the preliminary races from the hotel terraces or from yachts in the harbor, while the Grimaldis enjoy the spectacle from their royal box.

Income generated by the casino, hotels, and restaurants suffered during the worldwide depression of the 1930s. The legalization of some forms of gambling in parts of France also cut into Monte-Carlo revenues. Monte-Carlo recovered from the hard times and continues to be the showcase of

the principality—and the entire Mediterranean coast. Gambling operations still provide an important source of income, but it now constitutes a lesser percentage of revenue.

The luxurious Hermitage Hotel is another hotel that the world's rich and famous choose to stay in when visiting Monaco.

NEW ECONOMIC FRONTIERS

When Prince Rainier III ascended the throne in 1949, he was determined to diversify the economy. He knew that income from the casino alone would not allow for the kind of growth he had in mind for Monaco. During his 56-year reign, Rainier used creative approaches to expand the economy and find new sources of revenue. The prince was remarkably successful and, by the year 2000, the casino's revenues amounted to only about 5 percent of the principality's income. Each of the following economic sectors now make important contributions to the economy.

NEW LAND, NEW INDUSTRIES Between 1966 and 1973 one of Prince Rainier's major projects was using landfill to create a sizeable expansion of Monaco's land area through land reclamation. The new 54 acres (22 ha) of land became the principality's industrial area. Foreign corporations have been invited to build small, nonpolluting industrial facilities. These include cosmetic, pharmaceutical, plastic, and precision medical equipment companies. The setting itself adds to the beauty of Monaco. The buildings are constructed in a garden setting, including the Princess Grace Rose Garden, and they face the sparkling Mediterranean. The companies provide jobs for local residents as well as tax revenues for the government.

The world's largest floating dike being tugged to the old Monaco port at La Condamine from Spain where it was made.

TOURISM From the beginning of his rule Prince Rainier sought ways to expand Monaco's tourism. By combining improved beach facilities with advertising campaigns all over the world, the principality now draws vacationers throughout the year. The prince's imaginative plan to have a floating dike built in Spain and towed into the harbor has doubled the port's capacity. The harbor is constantly filled with yachts and sailboats, and the berths for cruise ships are among the finest in the world.

Hotels, restaurants, and shops, as well as beach and harbor facilities all provide jobs for local residents. Jobs include standard hotel and restaurant positions, managerial posts, and many support services, such as delivery, food supplies, and limousine services. Tourism is now Monaco's leading industry, drawing an estimated 700,000 visitors a year.

OTHER SOURCES OF REVENUE Monaco's refusal to have an income tax caused considerable friction with France in the years after World War II because wealthy French people and businesses were moving to Monaco in order to avoid France's income tax. Prince Rainier III finally relented and reached an agreement with the French government in 1962 to 1963. French citizens who became residents after January 1957 must pay French income tax. And Monaco companies that do more than 25 percent of their business outside of Monaco also must pay taxes. These taxes provide one of the government's sources of income.

Monaco receives income from several other sources: The principality has a monopoly on tobacco, the telephone network, and the postal service. Slightly more than half the annual revenue comes from taxes on hotels, restaurant meals, banks, and industries. Monaco's postage stamps

have been popular for years with collectors and tourists; the state holds a monopoly on their manufacture and sale.

Another important source of income—and employment—is provided by foreign companies that have established offices in Monaco to take advantage of the principality's low tax rates. To service these companies the city-state provides outstanding banking and other financial services. These services, of course, are also available to Monaco's wealthy citizens. The principality also operates its own radio and television networks, although the television transmitter had to be situated on Mount Agel in France to achieve the necessary height.

LOOKING AHEAD

With its varied sources of income, Monaco has become remarkably prosperous. The people enjoy one of the highest standards of living in the world, with annual per capita income equivalent to about $27,000. The beauty of the principality, with its varied architecture and many lush gardens, causes it to remain an unusually attractive place to live and work or just to visit.

The principality's ruling family and the National Council continue to look for ways to improve and expand the economy. The most important plan currently under consideration calls for building farther out into the Mediterranean Sea. Both the floating dike and the Fontvieille landfill were possible because international law allows every sovereign nation to control 12 miles (19 km) of sea and seabed off its shore. Monaco has hired experts to plan the building of three offshore islands. Each would be mounted on what is called a *tour de la mer*—a strong column that would be anchored to the seabed. Serious problems have to be overcome, such as the fact that the floor of the sea drops off sharply not far from the coast. If these difficulties can be overcome, Monaco will have more land area for businesses, gardens, and tourist attractions.

Opposite: **Monaco's stamps have also provided an unlikely source of revenue for the country due to their popularity among stamp collectors.**

Below: **A giant dock being towed to Monaco from Algeciras port in Spain. The huge structure took three years to build.**

ENVIRONMENT

WHEN PRINCE ALBERT II SUCCEEDED his father Rainier in 2005, one of his first acts was to sign the Kyoto Protocol. Each nation that signs the protocol agrees to reduce the amount of greenhouse emissions in their nation as a way of protecting the world's ozone. Only a handful of countries, including the United States, have refused to ratify the protocol, arguing that reducing emissions will harm the economy and result in loss of jobs.

The announcement of the signing surprised many people around the world, and in Monaco. Most people expected the prince to follow in the footsteps of his father, Prince Rainier III, who had devoted his energies to diversifying and expanding the economy. Instead, Prince Albert II was going on record saying that tiny Monaco would be a model in the worldwide struggle to reverse the destruction of the planet's air, water, land, and quality of life. The signing of the Kyoto Protocol was the first of several surprises the 48-year-old prince presented to the world.

Left: **Prince Albert II at the Earth Summit Plus 5 at the United Nations. He is greeted by Nane Annan, wife of Kofi Annan.**

Opposite: **The displays at the Oceanographic museum help to educate the public on the effects of the ocean on Monaco.**

Prince Albert II with certificate confirming his arrival to the geographical North Pole.

THE NORTH POLE AND GLOBAL WARMING

On April 16, 2006 newspapers around the world printed this news headline: "Monaco's Ruler Reaches North Pole." The subhead read: "Monaco's Prince Albert has reached the North Pole on his four-day expedition to highlight global warming."

The trip was carefully orchestrated and the prince held several news conferences in the month prior to the actual journey to the pole. He knew that the idea of the ruler of a Mediterranean resort principality traveling to the Arctic cold would draw the attention of curious journalists. It did, and Prince Albert II made the most of it. In a press conference he explained, "If in our modest way, by this action we are able to bring environmental problems to the forefront and force some leaders to take stronger actions, this expedition will have achieved its objectives."

Prince Albert II's great-great-grandfather, Prince Albert I, had made four Arctic trips in the early 1900s, but the current prince's venture was the first North Pole journey by any head of state while in office. On the last leg of the journey Prince Albert II left the expedition's base camp in Russia on April 12, 2006, for the four-day dash to the Pole. He led a team of seven, traveling by dogsled. The prince said it was a "physically difficult" journey. Two members of the team fell into the icy waters, but thankfully both were uninjured. The prince planted a flag of Monaco, as well as a flag of the International Olympic Committee, of which he is a member, at the North Pole.

On the day of his return to his camp, Prince Albert II used the publicity to hammer home his message. He talked about seeing evidence of global warming, such as shrinking glaciers. "We must try to find solutions [to global warming]," he said at a press conference, "with scientists, obviously, but also at the individual level. . . . I think everyone, by their behavior can make small contributions to a global and extraordinary effort."

FONDATION
PRINCE ALBERT II DE MONACO

Prince Albert at a press conference concerning his environmental foundation, which bears testament to his personal commitment to the environment.

A SPECIAL FUND

Another of Prince Albert II's initiatives has been helping to start a new investment program called a socially responsible investing fund. The program, which involves banks, investment firms, and the Monaco Environment Development Durable (MEDD), includes foreign as well as domestic institutions. Behind the many agencies and initials is a simple idea: to steer investment funds into such areas as renewable energy and healthy foods.

Leaders of environmental organizations have praised Prince Albert II for this initiative. As one said, "Prince Albert was the driving force behind the creation and the launch of this fund—it's really the reflection of his desire to contribute to the movement toward global sustainability." Corporations that receive funds are usually small firms that are striving to develop products that are not harmful to the environment or to humans.

The funds committed by MEDD are designed to return a small interest income to the prince. However, most observers agree that the primary goal is to encourage investment in sustainable growth, rather than in short-term growth at the expense of consumers' health or the environment.

URBAN ISSUES

In many ways Monaco is a small city, although it is also a sovereign state with the same rights and responsibilities as nations that are hundreds of times larger. Since it has no polluting industries and no runoff from agricultural lands, the principality has avoided many of the environmental problems faced by most larger countries. But Monaco does face several familiar environmental issues.

One problem is urban crowding. In technical terms Monaco is the world's most densely populated country. However, practically all countries appear less crowded because forests, farm regions, and other open areas change the statistics. In comparison to other countries around the world, Monaco is actually not as crowded. Nevertheless, issues such as vehicular emissions, sewage, and garbage removal are causes for concern. The principality has made agreements with French companies to provide sewage treatment and landfills for garbage. There are also strict rules for recycling, and recycled materials are also sent to France.

Monaco is one of the most densely populated countries in the world.

A giant inflatable whale was erected outside the Monaco Casino during the International Whaling Commission.

MONACO AND THE SEA

Monaco occupies less than one square mile of land between the Mediterranean Sea and the mountains. This has made the people and the government keenly aware of how changes in the world's oceans can affect their small city-state. In trying to alert world leaders to the dangers of global warming, Prince Albert II points out that as the world's ice caps continue to melt at an unprecedented rate, the melting ice will cause a rise in ocean levels that may be disastrous to coastal cities throughout the world.

In addition to the efforts of Prince Albert II, Monaco's Oceanographic Museum has been playing an important role in matters relating to the Mediterranean Sea and the world's oceans. The museum was built in the early 1900s by Prince Albert I. It is a large and impressive structure built against the face of a 250-foot (76-m) cliff. The museum's aquarium has living displays of more than 450 Mediterranean and tropical species.

The famous oceanographer and cinematographer Jacques-Yves Cousteau directed the museum for some 30 years, and his films are still shown in the lecture hall. Below the aquarium are the research laboratories that were used by Cousteau and a revolving team of scientists. In 1984 it was in the waters beneath the laboratories that Cousteau's scientists identified a fast-growing algae, nicknamed the "killer algae" because it blocks the sunlight from reaching native plants. Although the discovery of the bright-green algae seemed timely, the algae was already spreading at a fantastic rate. The killer algae originated in the Pacific Ocean and has now covered a huge area along the coast from Toulon to Menton. The museum's scientists are working with specialists from several countries to reverse the spread of the algae without harming other plant life.

Killer algae on the seabed of the Mediterranean poses serious problems for marine life there.

MONÉGASQUES

AS A COUNTRY, MONACO HAS THE distinction of being the world's most densely populated. As a city, however, which is what Monaco really is, it is not particularly crowded. Roughly 32,500 people live in an area of less than one square mile. Portions of other cities throughout the world, including New York, London, and Paris, hold larger numbers in neighborhoods of one square mile.

An unusual feature of the principality's population is that the native people, called Monégasques, are a minority, making up only 19 percent of the total population. French nationals, including those who have lived in Monaco for less than five years, make up close to a majority of the population at 32 percent. Italians make up another 20 percent. Other national and ethnic minorities, including Americans, constitute 29 percent.

Above: **The population of Monaco Is so varled that it is difficult to pinpoint native Monégasques.**

Opposite: **A Monégasque relaxing on his yacht.**

Apart from the roughly 6,000 Monégasques, it is difficult to define exactly who the people of Monaco are. The picture is complicated by the fact that some newcomers, who originally came to take advantage of the low tax rate on corporations, stay to become permanent residents, but it may be several years before their residency becomes official. In addition the national and ethnic makeup of the population reflects a history of people moving into the area over many centuries.

CENTURIES OF POPULATION MIXING

Monaco, including the coastal regions to the east (Menton and Roquebrune), has been home to a wide variety of people. Settlers from ancient Greece moved in between 600 B.C. and 400 B.C. establishing a trading colony named Monoikos. Around 125 B.C., the Romans began a gradual takeover of the entire Mediterranean coastal region. They made Monoikos Rome's first provincial (province), which gave the name Provence to this area of southern France. Some of the earliest architecture in greater Monaco dates from the Roman period, including the foundations of fortresses and the remains of amphitheaters and roads.

Following the collapse of the Roman Empire in the late 5th century, various Germanic tribes, including the Visigoths and Ostrogoths, invaded the area, destroying many towns and Roman buildings. Some of the invaders who originally came from eastern Europe and western Asia remained and intermarried with the local populations.

Around A.D. 1000, Italian city-states took control of much of the Mediterranean coast. While the Guelph and Ghibelline parties vied for control of the Monaco area, families from Genoa moved in. Some

A Roman arch in Vaucluse, Provence in France, is evidence of the Roman presence in the area.

remained in separate Genoese enclaves, while others mixed with the Monégasque population. Many Monégasques today continue to speak a dialect that is based on Genoese Italian. The Grimaldi family, one of the powerful clans of Genoa, became the ruling family of Monaco.

The Grimaldi realm included Menton and Roquebrune, as well as Monaco itself. This realm was prosperous from the 14th century through the late 18th century. The government relied on revenue obtained from taxing the area's lemons, oranges, and olive oil. As the taxes became an increasingly heavy burden, the people of Menton and Roquebrune began to rebel, some wanting independence and others preferring to be annexed by France.

Following the French Revolution, which began in 1789, the revolutionary French government captured Monaco and imprisoned the Grimaldi royal family. Monégasques hated French rule, which closed churches and turned them into "Temples of Reason." In 1815, after the fall of Napoleon, the Grimaldis once again ruled greater Monaco, although the region was placed under the protection of the king of Sardinia. Although few French people remained in Monaco after the revolutionary era, they left behind a legacy of strong Monégasque patriotism. Even today Monégasques insist that they are not part of France, but instead have their own distinct history and culture.

The King of Sardinia, Victor Emmanuel I took control over Monaco in 1815.

69

Today, the population of Monaco is made up of people from many different cultures.

MODERN DEMOGRAPHICS

The population of Monaco changed dramatically from the mid-1800s through the 1900s. First, Monaco lost 90 percent of its territory when the region of Menton-Roquebrune pulled away in 1848 and the Grimaldis recognized the area as part of France in 1861. The loss of this area removed the Grimaldis' major source of revenue and also a sizeable portion of Monaco's population, including people of both Italian and French descent.

The makeup of the population of Monaco proper also began to change. One major change came from the emergence of Monaco and the Mediterranean coast as a great resort area. Until the mid-1800s, swimming and sunbathing were virtually unknown anywhere in the world. A new trend may have been started by Tobias Smollett (1721–71), a famous English physician and novelist. On a visit to the coast about 6 miles (9.7 km) west of Monaco in 1763 Smollett took the extraordinary action of bathing in the Mediterranean Sea, part of his search for a cure to what was probably tuberculosis. He then wrote about his experience and urged others, including women, to follow his lead.

The idea of sea-bathing and vacationing on the coast was given an additional push by another famous Englishman, Henry Lord Brougham (1778–1868). Brougham built a large villa in Cannes, France, in 1834, and publicized the area as ideal for health and vacationing. Over the next 50 years, no less than 50 hotels were built, catering to wealthy Europeans.

Also in the mid-1800s, a guidebook named the entire coastal area the Côte d'Azur (Azure Coast). The name stuck; it seemed to be a perfect label for the deep blue of the usually cloudless sky. The same region was also called the French Riviera, and both names added luster to the coast and served to attract more and more people. By the 1890s a vacation on the Côte d'Azur became the favored destination for wealthy Europeans. When England's famous monarch Queen Victoria began to spend winters near Nice (9 miles [14.5 km] from Monaco) in the 1880s the advertising picture was complete.

The Cote d' Azur. Many people are attracted to its sapphire waters, clear skies, and mild climate.

As more and more people flocked to the Côte d'Azur or French Riviera, including Monaco, they added new elements to the population. The opening of Monaco's Monte Carlo Casino in 1863 encouraged some wealthy people to settle in Monaco, adding English, Germans, Italians, and Russians to the principality's population. A few wealthy Americans also discovered Monaco, including railroad tycoons like the Vanderbilts and Goulds.

Artists were also drawn to Monaco and the surrounding area by the intensity and clarity of the light and the picturesque views of countless villages. Matisse, Renoir, and other great Impressionists settled in the area, some permanently. Later, renowned artists like Pablo Picasso and Cocteau designed sets for Les Ballets de Monte-Carlo.

In the 20th century some of the Americans who settled in Monaco were drawn by literary figures who lived there, at least on a part-time basis. F. Scott Fitzgerald and H. G. Wells were among the writers who helped make Monaco a popular place to live. Sports figures and entertainers have also moved there part-time, adding to the allure. Leonardo DiCaprio and singer-philanthropist Bono are among other celebrities who have bought homes just outside Monaco, as did earlier figures such as John Wayne and Humphrey Bogart.

Many of the wealthy and famous people who have moved to Monaco have taken up permanent residency, aided by the comfortable tax laws. They are part of a population that is unlike that of any other country. People from France, Italy, England, the United States, the former Soviet Union, and other places account for an astonishing 80 percent of Monaco's population.

MONACO'S ROYAL FAMILY

Today the royal family of Monaco consists of the three children of Princess Grace and Prince Rainier III. Their middle child and only son, Prince Albert II, is the current ruler. Although he was regarded as a happy-go-lucky playboy he trained himself well to be the head of government. After attending college in the United States he worked for several U.S.-based global companies. This gave him an opportunity to study the workings of international trade and finance. He also displayed both skill and leadership in his love of athletics. He earned a black belt in judo, was team captain on the national soccer team, and was a champion in fencing. He is regarded as one of the "world's most eligible bachelors."

Princess Caroline (*below left*) is the oldest of the three children, born on January 23, 1957. After their mother, Princess Grace, died in 1982, Caroline stood in for her mother at royal functions. After Caroline's husband was killed in a boating accident in 1990 she withdrew from public life for a time, but gradually resumed her duties. In 1999 she married Prince Ernst of Hanover. She has been a patron of the arts, promoting dance and ballet.

Princess Stephanie was born on February 1, 1965. She was the most rebellious member of the royal family and her escapades were frequently reported in the scandal magazines. She has had several careers, including photographer, model, and fashion designer. She started her own perfume business, and more recently, launched a swimsuit line. Although divorced, she devotes much of her time to her three children.

Opposite: **The famous artist Pablo Picasso, who lived in Monaco and designed stage sets for the Les Ballets de Monte-Carlo.**

LIFESTYLE

THE LIFESTYLE IN MONACO IS NOT like that of any other country. It is based on extraordinary wealth and luxury. With one of the highest income levels of any country, Monaco has no poverty and virtually no unemployment. People who work in service jobs, such as servants, store clerks, and maintenance workers, live in towns outside the principality, or in the city of Nice, only 9 miles (14.5 km) to the west.

Many Monégasque families live much like modestly well-to-do families in other cities of Europe or America. Those who were born in Monaco, or who have lived here for at least five years, enjoy the city-state's status as a tax haven. Depending on their income level, people who do not have to pay income taxes can see their income rise by 40 to 50 percent.

Although there is no typical lifestyle in Monaco, the following two sections will give you a glimpse of how two large segments of the population live.

Left: **Many Monégasques like to bring tourists to street cafés like this to enjoy the scenery or people watch.**

Opposite: **A man tending to one of Monaco's many luscious and beautiful gardens.**

A MIDDLE-INCOME FAMILY

An average middle-income family usually consists of two parents and two children. Many of these middle-income families take up residence in high-rise apartments that sometimes overlook Monaco's harbor. This part of the city feels crowded, with large apartment buildings standing shoulder-to-shoulder on the steep hillside. From the harbor the city presents a wall of high-rises. Many adult Monégasques work in managerial positions for manufacturing companies or in the service industry, supporting Monaco's main tourism industry. Children attend schools locally or in boarding schools abroad.

Middle-income parents take turns preparing meals and the family usually eats together on their apartment's wrought-iron balcony with its great view of the yacht-filled harbor and white sails beyond. Breakfast normally consists of fruit or juice, a roll or croissant, and coffee or café au lait. Working adults usually have their midday meal at a restaurant, while schoolchildren eat in school. The family usually eats dinner at home. Dinner

is often a light affair comprising fresh greens, cheese, sausages, French bread, and sometimes, wine. The responsibility of shopping at the covered marketplace is alternated between the parents. The covered marketplace is jammed with colorful stalls of flowers, herbs, fruits, and vegetables.

Many Monégasques bring their tourist friends for lunch at famous restaurants surrounded by lush gardens. They are well-known for "people watching," as passengers from cruise ships stroll past to go shopping. Monégasques and tourists alike like to shop in the neighborhood called the Golden Circle, where exclusive shops feature clothing, jewelry, and cosmetics from every famous designer in Paris, Rome, London, and New York.

For some light exercise, Monégasques may spend an hour walking through the Jardins du Casino, the luxurious green area surrounding the famous casino. Some people extend their encounter with nature by hiking along the coastal road that extends from Monte-Carlo east to Roquebrune and beyond.

THE UPSCALE LIFESTYLE

The lure of the Monte-Carlo casino in the mid-1800s, along with Monaco's most lavish hotels and restaurants, brought hundreds of the wealthiest Europeans to the principality. This glittering era became known as the belle époque (the beautiful epoch). It continued in the early 20th century, with the influx of Hollywood stars and sports figures. The lifestyle of the rich and famous continues in Monaco today.

Many of the wealthy Monégasques or residents own yachts, and many of these are extravagant enough to have their own helicopter pads. Homes are also luxurious, ranging from multimillion-dollar apartments to villas with a dozen bedrooms. Most of these homes have staffs of maids,

Some of the wealthier members of Monégasque society taking advantage of the beautiful Mediterranean.

cooks, gardeners, and servants. Some wealthy people are employed, including opera stars and singers; sports figures, including Grand Prix race drivers; and stars of films and television. Others are bankers or investors and retired owners of businesses.

Most of Monaco's wealthy lead a cushioned lifestyle, with servants to take care of many of their physical needs. But many also devote some of their time and money to worthwhile causes, such as environmental protection, saving wildlife, and a variety of charities. One of the most important annual events, for example, is the Red Cross Gala Ball, held in early August. Prince Albert II, along with his sisters, the princesses Stephanie and Caroline, welcome guests to the *salle des étoiles* of the Sporting d'Eté club. This is one of Europe's largest charity events, with more than 1,000 guests paying more than $1,000 each to attend.

Performers at the 58th Annual Red Cross Gala Ball.

Grand old houses in Old Town Monaco can cost millions of dollars. Some of the rich and famous of the world take up residence in houses like this.

CATERING TO THE RICH AND FAMOUS

Maintaining the upscale lifestyle requires the support of many organizations, institutions, and events. For example, wearing the right clothing and presenting the most attractive appearance involve effort and money. Many people attend a show called *Destination Bien-Etre* (The Goal of Well-Being) in Fontvieille. The show is devoted to both beauty and health. Specialists in several fields, such as skin care and nutrition, conduct workshops. A variety of massages and physical therapies are also scheduled throughout the day, leaving time for shopping.

Another event designed to help people maximize their luxurious lifestyle is the annual Monaco Yacht Show, held in September. Nearly 550 companies display yachting merchandise to more than 15,000 people. Visitors can board yachts and view hundreds of glistening accessories.

A full dress ballet rehearsal at the Princess Grace Academy of Classical Dance.

EDUCATION AND HEALTH

Education is free and compulsory for children aged 6 to 16. Literacy rates are high, standing at about 99 percent. There are a number of elementary schools, a junior high school, a senior high school, and three private schools. A total of nearly 6,000 students are served by these schools.

Although many students go on to colleges in France there are some specialized schools in Monaco. The Technical Lycée of Monte Carlo offers training in hotel and restaurant management, as well as technical and commercial courses, such as accounting, banking, and computer programming. Other specialized schools include the Princess Grace Academy of Classical Dance and the Rainier III Academy of Music.

Health standards are high, and that is reflected in the statistics for life expectancy in Monaco. Life expectancy at birth is 75.7 years for men and 83.6 years for women. Most doctors receive their training in France or other European countries. Princess Grace Hospital is a modern facility with the most advanced equipment and treatments.

RELIGION

ON ANY GIVEN DAY THE STREETS OF Monaco are likely to be crowded with people participating in a religious festival. Or, if a religious celebration is not in progress, then one has probably just ended or is about to begin. The people of Monaco enjoy their religion and they eagerly participate in the many holy days on the year's calendar. Some observances are somber affairs, involving quiet processions to a church or the cathedral. But most are joyous celebrations, with lots of music and dancing, food and beverages, and people wearing colorful traditional costumes.

The majority of Monégasques are Catholic, with more than 90 percent of the people listing themselves as members of the Roman Catholic Church. Catholicism is the country's official religion, but the constitution guarantees freedom of religion. About 5 percent of the population belongs to one of the Protestant religions, with Episcopalians being the most numerous.

Left: **Catholic processions like this are common during religious festivals.**

Opposite: **A Catholic priest conducting Mass at the Palatine Chapel.**

The Monaco cathedral was constructed in 1875 out of white stones. The tombs of the deceased princes of Monaco are housed here.

JEWS AND MUSLIMS

Monaco has been home to a small number of Jews for many centuries. Before and during World War II (1939–45), hundreds of Jewish refugees came from other parts of Europe, attempting to escape persecution by Nazi-controlled Germany. Monégasque officials tried to help Jews by providing fake documents, but Nazi agents discovered many of the refugees. The Nazis kidnapped several hundred and sent them to concentration camps, where many died.

A few Jews continue to live in Monaco today, including several families. There is no synagogue, however, so religious services are conducted in people's homes and led by lay leaders (rather than ordained rabbis). There is also a small number of Muslims, most of them from North African countries. There are also frequent business visitors from the oil-producing states of the Persian Gulf, such as Kuwait and Saudi Arabia. There are no mosques for these part-time residents, most of whom come to take advantage of Monaco's tax-free banking facilities.

FESTIVALS AND HOLY DAYS

There are religious festivals and holy days in almost every month of the year. Late January marks the Feast of Saint Dévote, Monaco's patron saint.

In the spring, Monégasques and other residents observe Lent, the 40 days leading up to Easter Sunday and Easter Monday. During Lent, many people go to daily Mass services to take part in the Stations of the Cross—symbolically retracing the pain-filled steps of Jesus on the way to the

Catholic priests performing Easter Mass, which marks the end of the period of Lent and celebrates the resurrection of Jesus Christ.

Crucifixion. The solemnity of Good Friday, with all church statues draped in mourning, is followed by the joyous music and prayers of Easter Sunday and Easter Monday.

On the days just before Ash Wednesday, which introduces the Lenten period of church services and partial fasting, the principality explodes with a celebration called Carnival. For two days, people engage in a round of parties, parades, and feasts. The event is much like Carnival, or Mardi Gras, in other countries, including the American city of New Orleans. At Monaco's Carnival, children dress in traditional costumes and march through the city.

Another popular religious festival celebrates Saint John's Day in June. On the eve of Saint John's Day, a crowd gathers on the Palace Square. A Monégasque folk group—the Palladienne—wear historical costumes and sing and dance, accompanied by music played on mandolins. The costumes consist of long, frilly shirts and garments with red and white stripes. The Palladienne are joined by folk groups from France, Italy, and Spain. Meanwhile, the royal family attends a service in the Palace Chapel, which is dedicated to Saint John the Baptist.

After the service, two footmen from the palace carry burning torches to the square, where they light a huge bonfire. Brave celebrants often leap through the flames. On Saint John's Day itself, a procession forms at Monte-Carlo. The folk groups create a guard around "Little Saint John" (or Saint Jean) and his lamb and march through the streets. Music, dancing, and eating continue far into the night.

MONACO'S PATRON SAINT

The roots of many religious practices go far back in time, some to the earliest days of Christianity, including the persecution of Christians in the third and fourth centuries by the Roman Empire. One of Monaco's favorite religious festivals—the Feast of Saint Dévote—dates from this era. Dévote is the patron saint of Monaco.

According to the ancient legend a young woman named Dévote, from the island of Corsica, was one of the victims of the Roman persecution in the early fourth century. Although she was tortured until she died Dévote refused to renounce her faith. To deny her a Christian burial the Romans placed her in a small dilapidated boat and set it adrift, assuming that it would soon sink in the depths of the Mediterranean.

The boat did not sink. Instead a dove flew out of the dead woman's mouth and gently blew the leaking boat to a cove in Monaco. Although it was winter a bush burst into blossom on the spot where the boat landed. Dévote was buried on January 27. Many sailors and fishing families began praying at her grave site. Several miracles were attributed to her and she was declared a saint by the Vatican.

Some years later thieves stole Dévote's bones, planning to sell them as religious relics (objects with special religious or healing powers). Some

sailors chased away the thieves, rescued the bones, and set the thieves' boat on fire. The Feast of Saint Dévote on January 27 celebrates Dévote as the principality's patron saint. The royal family participates in the ceremonies, and the ruling prince puts a torch to a small boat, reenacting the burning of the thieves' boat.

In the 11th century a stately chapel was built on the spot where Dévote's boat landed. After a service in the chapel, during which the town and the harbor are blessed, the celebration includes the releasing of doves and a fireworks display in the harbor.

The late Prince Rainier III setting fire to a boat in honor of Monaco's patron saint, Saint Devoté.

OTHER RELIGIOUS OBSERVANCES

In addition to Dévote, Monégasques also celebrate another martyred figure—Saint Roman. Roman was a soldier in the army of the Roman Empire and was an early convert to Christianity. In the year 258 he was ordered to renounce his faith and, when he refused, he was executed. Like Dévote he became one of the Christian martyrs and was elevated to sainthood. His feast day, August 9, is celebrated with ancient hymns and a procession.

A number of holy days and festivals are spread throughout the year. Many are more typical of Roman Catholic observances, but some include local or regional traditions.

Epiphany, for example, is celebrated on January 6, between New Year's Day and the Feast of Saint Dévote. People usually buy a *galette des rois*

A procession during the Festival of Saint Dévote.

Details of a painting of the Virgin Mary ascending to heaven in a painting by Giuseppe Ghedine.

(king's cake), a puff pastry with a creamy filling. The person who finds the *feve* (a bean) receives a crown and a reward. (The bean embedded in the cake is now usually a plastic or porcelain figurine.)

During the period before Easter a number of men in an organization called the Venerable Brotherhood of Black Penitents of Mercy hold special services. Dressed in black they have a procession that reenacts the Stations of the Cross. The organization dates back to the Crusades, when Christians tried to capture the Holy Land. They conclude the ceremony with services at the Chapel of Mercy, built in the early 1600s.

Other traditional holy days include Pentecost, or Whitsunday, on the seventh Sunday after Easter. It celebrates the descent of the Holy Spirit upon the disciples. This is followed by the Feast of the Ascension, on the 40th day after Easter, celebrating Christ's ascent into Heaven. On August 15,

Christmas decorations in Monaco lend a festive air throughout the principality.

Catholics observe the Feast of the Assumption, celebrating the bodily taking of the Virgin Mary into Heaven following her death.

November 1 is All Saints' Day, when the church celebrates all the saints. Another religious feast day is December 8, the Feast of the Immaculate Conception. According to Catholic beliefs, this is when the Virgin Mary herself was conceived without original sin.

Christmas celebrations vary, depending partly on where family traditions originated. Many Monégasques, for example, still follow an ancient tradition in which a young family member—either a boy or a girl—dips an olive branch into a glass of wine. The child then stands in front of the fireplace and makes the sign of the Cross with the olive branch, while reciting a poem that glorifies the olive tree. Everyone then takes a sip of the wine before enjoying a meal of traditional Monégasque foods. One of those foods is usually *fougasses*—flat, crispy bread sprinkled with red and white aniseed.

LANGUAGE

FRENCH IS THE DOMINANT LANGUAGE of Monaco, used for writing as well as reading. There is also a local Monégasque language, or dialect. Courses in Monégasque are still taught in the schools, but it is used by only about 15 percent of the population. It is a combination of French and Italian, with a few words from the language of Genoa, dating back to the Middle Ages. Most people also speak at least some English.

A generation ago Monégasque was no longer being taught in the schools and the language was in danger of becoming extinct. Around 1980 a revival was started by the government of Prince Rainier III. This was part of a broader effort to build greater pride in Monaco's cultural heritage.

Opposite: **Road signs printed in French, the working language of Monaco.**

Below: **Many Monégasques enjoy chatting with their friends over a cup of coffee at street cafés.**

PRONOUNCING FRENCH WORDS

Most letters are pronounced much like letters in English. But there are some special cases and a few general rules that are helpful.

Emphasize each syllable, but do not pronounce the last consonant of a word—including the plural *s*.

The letter *c* is pronounced like an English *k* when it comes before *a*, *o*, or *u*.

Before *e* and *i*, it is pronounced like the *s* in "sun".

The letter *h* is always silent.

The letter *j* is pronounced like the *s* in "leisure," and it is often written as *zh*.

The letter *r* is pronounced from the back of the throat to roll it. (This comes with practice and listening.)

When a syllable ends in an *n* or *m*, these letters are not pronounced, but the vowel that comes before them is given a nasal pronunciation.

The letter *s* is often not pronounced in plurals or at the end of words.

The pronouns *vous* and *tu* can be troublesome for visitors and newcomers. Both mean "you" but *tu* is a more intimate word. It is used to refer to someone you know very well or when speaking to children or animals. When addressing any adult who is not a close friend, one should always use *vous*. Trouble arises when visitors, especially Americans, in an effort to be friendly, use *tu* too readily, even with people they have just met.

Due to its strong influence from neighboring France, most Monégasques speak French.

THE SILENT LANGUAGE

Sometimes actions and even facial expressions can communicate just as well as spoken words. Anthropologist Edward T. Hall called this nonverbal communication "the silent language."

Like the people of southern France, for example, Monégasques often gesture a good deal with their hands as they talk. Visitors sometimes get the impression that the person is very emotional, or overly excited.

Similarly, when people in Monaco greet one another, they kiss each other on the cheek, usually once or twice, but three kisses are considered appropriate. This is another case where a visitor may inadvertently be offended.

Choosing the wrong word is another way in which misunderstandings can occur. When introducing a Monégasque to another person, saying only the person's name may seem overly familiar. To be on the safe side, travel consultants say, it is always best to introduce the person as Madame, Monsieur, or Mademoiselle, followed by their name.

Well-meaning visitors can sometimes use a wrong term to address someone and unwittingly cause a misunderstanding.

Another common mistake is made by visitors who know that the French word *garçon* means "boy," however, it can also refer to a waiter in a restaurant. Summoning a waiter by calling out "*garçon*," however, can be an insult to the waiter, who does not want to be referred to as "boy."

SAMPLE WORDS AND PHRASES

English	French
Excuse me.	*Pardon, excusez-moi.*
Thank you (very much).	*Merci (beaucoup).*
How are you?	*Comment allez-vous?*
Fine.	*Ça va bien.*
I don't understand.	*Je ne comprends pas.*
I don't know.	*Je ne sais pas.*
Could you speak more slowly?	*Pourriez-vous parler plus lentement?*
What time is it?	*Quelle heure-est-il?*
It's (8) o'clock.	*Il est (huit) heures.*
No problem.	*Pas de probleme.*
That's it!	*C'est ça!*
There it is!	*Voila!*
Here it is!	*Voici!*
Let's go.	*On y va or Allons-y.*
See you tomorrow.	*A demain.*
See you soon.	*Bientôt.*
Okay.	*D'accord.*

STREET SIGNS

Street and traffic signs are often printed in both French and English. A sign written only in French can lead to confusion. Here are some examples:

French	English
Cédez la Priorité	Yield, or give way
Défense de Stationner	No parking
Interdiction de Doubler	Do not pass
Ralentissez	Slow down
Sens Unique	One way
Entrée	Entrance
Sens Interdit	One way street, no entry or entrance
Sortie	Exit

SAMPLES OF MONACO'S FOUR LANGUAGES

You can hear all of these languages on the streets of Monaco:

English	French	Monégasque	Italian
Hello	*Bonjour*	*Salve*	*Buongiorno*
Good-bye	*Au revoir*	*A se revede*	*Arrivederci*
My name is	*Je m'appelle*	*Me ciamu*	*Mi chiamo*
Please	*S'il vous plait*	*Per pieijé*	*Per favor*
Thank you	*Merci*	*Merçi*	*Grazie*
Yes	*Oui*	*Sci*	*Si*
Sir	*Monsieur*	*Sciü* (or *Monsue*)	*Signore*
Madam	*Madame*	*Sciá* (or *Madama*)	*Signora*

Hommage des Colonies Etrangères
à S.A.S. le Prince Albert Ier
à l'occasion de ses XXV années de règne

ARTS

IN SPITE OF ITS SMALL SIZE Monaco has established an outstanding reputation in the arts, especially in music and dance. The royal family has worked hard to build and maintain that reputation. Numerous annual festivals and awards draw artists and performance groups from all parts of the world. Prince Rainier III and Princess Grace were especially active patrons of the arts. They both started art foundations that have continued their respective contributions in the 21st century.

The principality is also well known for its art facilities. Some concerts and performances are held in beautiful outdoor settings, surrounded by lush gardens with picturesque views of the harbor and the Mediterranean. Other performances are held in buildings famous for their architecture.

Left: **The enjoyment of music is by no means exclusive to the elite of Monaco. Street bands like this add to the atmosphere of the country.**

Opposite: **A statue in commemoraton of Prince Rainier's rule of Monaco.**

MUSIC AND DANCE

The famous Monte-Carlo casino was designed by French architect Charles Garnier, and it includes the Salle Garnier, an elaborate red and gold structure that is home to the Monte-Carlo Opera, the Ballets de Monte-Carlo, and the 100-member Monte-Carlo Philharmonic Orchestra. The building, which has just been renovated, was inaugurated with a performance by the renowned Sarah Bernhardt in 1879, and has welcomed guest artists from Enrico Caruso in the early 1900s to contemporary singers, including Luciano Pavarotti, Plácido Domingo, and Andrea Bocelli. The Ballet Russes de Monte-Carlo, a company formed prior to Les Ballets de Monte-Carlo, has also seen performances by every major dancer of the late 19th and 20th century. Famous composers, such as Igor Stravinsky, have written pieces for it, and sets have been designed by artists such as Jean Cocteau and Pablo Picasso.

The Monte-Carlo Philharmonic Orchestra usually performs in the Monte-Carlo Opera House but in summer it plays in the Palace Courtyard. The orchestra also acts as one of Monaco's goodwill ambassadors by playing in other countries.

A boys' choir also represents Monaco in the world. The choir, named Les Petits Chanteurs de Monaco (The Little Singers of Monaco) was originally formed by Prince Antoine I in the early 18th century to sing liturgical music in the Palatine Chapel. Prince Rainier III revived the choir in the early 1970s. It consists of about 30 young singers from Monaco, France, and Italy. Twice a year the boys go on tours of other countries. For most of the year they sing at 10:00 A.M. Mass at the cathedral.

Throughout the year, visitors and Monégasques enjoy a wide variety of music in addition to the classical forms. During the summer months, for

Opposite: **Two girls rehearse at Monaco's Academie du Danse.**

Below: **Prince Albert II and his entourage at the Monte-Carlo Opera House.**

Opposite: **Ceiling painting of the Palatine Chapel. The chapel was built in the 17th century under the rule of Prince Honoré II and was restored two centuries later by Prince Charles III.**

example, the Monte-Carlo Sporting Club holds concerts by internationally known recording stars. Now in its 34th year, the club's past performers have included David Bowie, Cher, Natalie Cole, and the Beach Boys. The club also puts on Las Vegas-style floor shows.

Numerous other concerts are held during the year, such as "Jazz on the Rock," which is held in September. In addition several nightclubs offer live jazz every evening, while others have rock groups or dance bands.

Another annual event is the Monte-Carlo Spring Arts Festival, usually held in April. The event includes classical and modern dance performances, concerts, and recitals. Events are held in numerous places and public squares, as well as the new Grimaldi Forum Monaco.

FOUNDATION CONTRIBUTIONS

The royal family makes great contributions to music, dance, and theater. With ample funds at their disposal, princes and princesses have formed foundations that enable them to channel funds in the most efficient ways.

The Princess Grace Foundation, for example, was formed by the princess in 1964 to provide aid to the arts, while also supporting medical and social programs. The foundation funds the Princess Grace Dance Academy, with classes and experimental performances in a lovely villa. Another activity supported by the foundation is the Princess Grace Irish Library.

In 1996 Prince Rainier III organized the Prince Pierre Foundation in honor of his father. This foundation awards several annual prizes, including the annual Grand Literary Prize, the Prince Rainier III Prize for Musical Composition, and the International Contemporary Art Prize. Another royal foundation is the Prince Rainier Musical Academy Foundation, which promotes new and even experimental pieces, and awards the Musical Composition Prize.

SCULPTURE AND ARCHITECTURE

The streets, gardens, and public squares of Monaco are always filled with beautiful colors and the sounds of many musical forms. Contributing to this feast for the senses are the many beautiful buildings and the striking fountains and sculptural works. In addition to the buildings designed by Charles Garnier there are splendid privately-owned villas, churches, palaces, and forts. Some structures have been modernized from their original form. The 18th-century Fort Antoine has become a popular theater that displays a wide range of productions in summer.

The construction of the largest church in Monaco, the Cathedral of the Immaculate Conception, began in 1875 and was built over a 10-year period. It is built out of elegant Italian marble, creating a massive, cream-colored façade. It is famous for its ancient altarpiece and

for being the burial place of many members of the royal family, including Princess Grace. A much smaller church, the Palatine Chapel, was originally built in the 13th century as the Chapel of Saint John the Baptist. It is known for its strikingly beautiful ceiling painting and stained glass windows.

Other well-known buildings include the magnificent Princely Palace, the National Museum that was designed by Garnier, the glass-walled Grimaldi Forum Monaco, with more than half the structure submerged beneath the surface of the sea, and the Oceanographic Museum, with its façade rising from a sheer cliff.

Like the beautiful architecture, striking sculptures seem to be everywhere. Every other year, from June to October, the Monte-Carlo International Sculpture Festival challenges sculptors with a theme for which they can submit works. All sorts of styles and materials are encouraged. The international panel of judges looks for originality and creative expression. The theme for 2006 was "The Walk Towards Life," which inspired submissions such as a statue of Adam and Eve and another of a giant pregnant woman.

Many of the prizewinners' works are put on public display. Monaco's many gardens offer a perfect setting for this. Outside the Oceanographic Museum, for example, the steep paths of the Saint Martin Gardens are studded with sculpture. The central strip of the Casino Garden serves a similar function, and the Princess Grace Rose Garden devotes a large pathway called Chemin des Sculptures (Sculpture Road) to sculptures, including some that are part of Monaco's permanent collection.

TELEVISION

In 1961 Prince Rainier III launched the first Monte Carlo Television Festival. In his introduction, the prince said that the purpose of the event was to "encourage a new form of artistic expression in the service of peace and understanding for mankind." The gathering was a pioneering effort, since regular television broadcasting had started barely a decade earlier.

Part of Rainier's plan was to add to Monaco's status in the world as a cultural leader. Television was seen as a way of bringing nations and cultures together and helping them acquire mutual understanding. The event was an immediate success. Many distinguished celebrities sit on juries to judge the best in television programming. The event is held every year in the Grimaldi Forum.

Above: **Actors Adrian Pasdar and Masi Oka at the 47th Monte-Carlo Television Awards promoting their new series** *Heroes.*

Opposite: **The Oceanographic Museum was designed by architect Paul Delefortrie (1843–1910) and took 11 years to build.**

LEISURE

LIFE IN MONACO SEEMS TO BE centered around leisure activities. In fact, many visitors think of the principality as a kind of high-priced, high-quality entertainment park. It is true that an amazing array of activities can be found in a very small area, including shopping, water sports, music and dance, theater and cinema, and a variety of sports for both participants and spectators.

Both residents and visitors expect to spend a lot of money to enjoy themselves, and leisure activities can be very expensive. On a typical day, for instance, a well-to-do young couple might first spend time (and money) visiting exclusive designer shops in the neighborhood known as the Carré d'Or (Golden Square). They might then dine in the posh 17th-century décor of the Louis XV restaurant, said to be the finest on the entire Riviera, followed by a pampering at a luxury spa, featuring a rose-scented massage. The evening could be spent at the fabled Monte-Carlo casino, where formal attire (and a good deal of money) is required.

At the other end of the economic scale, however, very little money is needed to experience a delightful day in Monaco. One could attend a noontime concert at the Parc Fontvieille, then dine on slices of pizza from the Casino Supermarket, while strolling through the Chemin des Sculptures in the Princess Grace Rose Garden. After a visit to any of the outstanding museums, visitors may choose to have a picnic with fresh foods from Monaco's covered market on the waterfront and, as the sun goes down, enjoy a display of Monaco's famous fireworks over the harbor.

Above: **Visitors can enjoy sculptures like this along the Chemin des Sculptures.**

Opposite: **A paraglider enjoys a thrilling experience over Monaco.**

The Philharmonic orchestra performing on the grounds of the Royal Palace.

ENTERTAINMENT

The rich assortment of music, dance, and theater programs makes up part of the entertainment listings available in Monaco. Movie theaters, although few in number, are popular. In summer the New Open-Air Cinema, which boasts the largest outdoor screen in all of Europe, shows English-language films. Monégasques are particularly fond of movies. A number of films have been shot here, including *To Catch a Thief*, the Alfred Hitchcock thriller that brought Grace Kelly to Monaco. In addition, many Hollywood personalities vacation in Monaco or nearby, especially when the prestigious Cannes Film Festival is in progress.

A variety of festivals offers different forms of entertainment throughout the year. The International Fireworks Festival fills the night sky in July and August with displays of fireworks by the leading pyrotechnic specialists from many countries. November brings the national holiday, for example, and the International Circus Festival arrives in January. Just about every month of the year offers yet another festival, filling the principality with a carnival-like atmosphere.

THE MONACO GRAND PRIX

The principality offers many outstanding events for spectators, but the most famous is the Formula One Grand Prix. The trophy is one that is most coveted by drivers and the race is definitely the most glamorous one on the circuit. It is made up of 17 Formula One races, held on four continents, leading to the finale in Brazil.

On a Sunday in late May, the air in Monaco is filled with the smell of high-powered fuel and burning rubber, as well as the roar of engines and the screeching of tires. The cars race through the very heart of the city, going uphill from the start/finish line to the casino, then streaking downhill around a tight hairpin turn and two other sharp turns and through a tunnel, along the harbor, navigating more sharp turns that lead back to the start/finish line. The cars have to run through this course 77 times before the race is considered complete.

Spectators watch the excitement from terrace restaurants or from people's homes, while the wealthy enjoy the comforts of the Hôtel Hermitage or view the race from luxury yachts in the harbor. The Grimaldis and their guests have a royal box at the port.

In terms of races, the Monaco Grand Prix is not considered to be one of the greatest by experts. For one thing the course is too tight and tricky

The Monaco Grand Prix is one of the most popular spectator events in Monaco.

Vintage cars in Monaco.

for the big Formula One cars, which are built for speed rather than sharp turns. (The average speed is only 88 miles per hour (about 142 km per hour). And, because of the many tight turns and steep hills, it is almost impossible to pass another car.

No other race, however, can compare with the Monaco Grand Prix for sheer excitement and glamour. And, for the Monaco spectators, the speed certainly does not seem too slow. In fact, until stronger barriers were erected, there were two incidences when cars plowed through the straw bales and into the harbor. (On both occasions, the drivers suffered only minor injuries.)

Many Formula One drivers make Monaco their permanent home. They include some of the most famous personalities in the racing world such as Emanuele Pirro and Mika Pauli Häkkinen.

OTHER AUTOMOBILE EVENTS

The fascination with cars is not limited to the Formula One Grand Prix. The Monte Carlo Rally, held in January every year, is another famous event. This is a three-day race, held in timed stages, which begins and ends in Monaco. In between it follows a tortuous route through Provence. The winding mountain roads above Monaco are sometimes clogged with snow.

January and February also witness the Monte Carlo Historic Car Rally. Historic sportscars take part in a race that begins in Valence, then follows a challenging course, with a pause in Gap, and finishes in Monaco.

Prince Rainier III was a race-car buff and a collector of historic cars. More than 100 of his vehicles are on display at the Collection de Voitures Anciennes (Collection of Classic Cars). The collection includes the Bugatti 1929, the winner of the first Monaco Grand Prix.

The calm Mediterranean waters surrounding Monaco encourage and attract many to take up boating.

A TOUR OF MONACO SPORTS

Prince Rainier III once said, "To be a true Monégasque, you must have a love of sports." Monaco offers a seemingly endless variety of sports. Here is a sampling.

BOATING AND BEACH ACTIVITIES Monaco Harbor is filled with a wide array of sailboats and yachts. There are numerous luxury yachts and many are anchored at the members-only Monaco Yacht Club, but all sorts of motor craft and sailboats enjoy the calm waters and magnificent views. Visitors can take tours in a glass-bottomed catamaran operated by a tour company. The adventurous can try deep-sea fishing for tuna, or join a sailboat race. Those who prefer observing or sightseeing can take a helicopter tour of the entire coast.

The Rainier III Nautical Stadium hosts Olympic-quality swimming races. A number of European and world records have been set here. Water polo matches and beach volleyball are also popular.

TENNIS AND GOLF   Visitors and full-time residents take advantage of Monaco's many tennis courts. People play for pleasure, to keep in shape, and for a variety of amateur competitions.

In the spring of every year, the Monte Carlo Country Club hosts the Tennis Masters Series. The best players in men's tennis compete in an event that celebrated its 100th edition in 2006. The Masters Series ranks second only to the Grand Slam in importance and prestige. The series consists of four tournaments in North America and five in Europe.

The Monte Carlo Pro-Celebrity PGA Golf Tournament is the major golfing event that is held at the Monte Carlo Golf Club. Outstanding professional golfers are paired with famous entertainers, including film stars. People who simply want to play golf at the Monte Carlo Golf Club need to make reservations a year or two in advance.

TEAM SPORTS Of the team sports, football (soccer) is by far the most popular. Young people play wherever they can find space; and the ultramodern, 20,000-seat Louis II Stadium in Fontvieille is the venue for European Junior matches and for French First Division matches. The

Top seed Roger Federer from Switzerland competing in the 2006 Monte Carlo Tennis Open.

Monégasque National Team is the pride and joy of the principality. In their red-and-white uniforms, they include players from France, Italy, and Monaco, as well as other countries. The team more than holds its own against such teams from Marseilles and Paris, but it has not yet performed well in World Cup competition.

Other team sports for watching or playing include bicycle races, squash, gymnastics, and handball. The Monaco Sports Association (ASM) works hard to develop interest in several other sports organizations, including the Archery Company, the Monaco Rifle Club, the Monaco Cycling Union, and, for rowers, the Société Nautique de Monaco.

PÉTANQUE Throughout the Riviera, including Monaco, an unusual game that is wildly popular is called *pétanque* or boules. (The Italian game of bocci is quite similar.) The game, with two to six players divided into two teams, is played on a level gravel course. Each player has three boules, made of solid metal, that weigh 1 pound, 7 ounces to 1 pound, 12 ounces (650 to 800 grams). Each team takes a turn rolling a boule at a small wooden ball called a *cochonnet* (jack), trying to land a boule as close to the *cochonnet* as possible. The team with the closest boule wins the round and earns one point. The first team to earn 13 points wins the match.

The toss is always made underhanded from inside a small circle scratched in the gravel. Both the player's feet are firmly planted on the ground. At the end of a round, a new circle is drawn around the *cochonnet* and the boules must be rolled from 6.6 to 11 yards (6 to 10 m) farther away.

There is now an international federation of *pétanque* national associations. There are more than 500,000 players registered, representing about 50 countries, including Canada and the United States. The world championship is often held in Monaco's Rainier III Boules Stadium.

MONACO AND WORLD SPORTS

Prince Rainier III and now Prince Albert II have devoted a good deal of energy and creativity to making their tiny principality stand out in the world of sports. Prince Albert, for example, has served on the International Olympics Committee for several years, and was also captain of Monaco's bobsled team in four Winter Olympics.

Under the leadership of Prince Rainier III, Monaco encouraged several international sports organizations to establish headquarters in the city. These organizations include the International Association for Sport Without Violence. Rainier helped to create the association and served as its president. In total, Monaco's Department of the Interior oversees the work of more than 50 sports organizations, many of which provide financial aid to promote various sports.

MUSEUMS AND PUBLIC GARDENS

Both residents and visitors can spend leisure hours in Monaco's outstanding museums and public gardens. The National Museum is located in a grand villa designed by Charles Garnier. It includes a huge doll collection and mechanical toys. Nearby, the Naval Museum showcases more than 200 model ships. There is also an elaborate gondola built for the Emperor Napoleon. The Princely Palace has more Napoleon-related items on display in the Museé des Souvenirs Napoléoniens et Archives Historiques du Palais (Musuem of Napoleonic Souvenirs and the Historic Archives of the Palace).

The Wax Museum of the Princes of Monaco offers 24 life-size figures in historic tableaux of the Grimaldi family history. A few steps away is a 17th-century chapel called the Musée de la Chapelle de la Visitation (Museum of the Chapel of the Visitation). In this wonderful setting there are artworks by some great masters, including Rubens.

Above: **The Whale Room in the Oceanographic Museum.**

Opposite: **The Japanese Gardens.**

The Oceanographic Museum is one of Monaco's most famous sites. Even the décor is sea-themed, including chandeliers shaped like seabirds and oak doorframes carved into marine shapes. The Whale Room contains skeletons and preserved specimens of whales and marine creatures. Outside the museum the plants of the Jardins Saint Martin cover the steep hillsides above the coast. The garden includes a number of lovely statues, as well as breathtaking views.

From the garden an outdoor escalator leads to a little theater that presents a half-hour film of the Monte Carlo Story. Visitors will find a display of historic film posters interesting and fun to view. Across the street visitors can take the Azur Express, a train that offers a 30-minute tour of the city, with an informative commentary in English.

FESTIVALS

AT TIMES MONACO SEEMS LIKE the land of festivals. Throughout the year Monégasques, other permanent residents, and visitors are treated to an almost constant round of festive celebrations. These begin in January with New Year's, the International Circus Festival, and the Feast of Saint Dévote. They continue through the year and conclude with Christmas Mass and celebrations in December.

There are at least two reasons for the many festivals. For one thing the people love a good party. An event that combines parades, music, colorful costumes, lots of food, and often, fireworks, has all the ingredients for a grand celebration. Another important reason for at least some of the festivals is that they provide a convenient way to bring visitors to

Left: **Many visitors travel to Monaco just to watch the Monte Carlo International Circus Festival.**

Opposite: **The circus parade on the streets of Monaco during the 30th circus festival.**

117

Prince Albert II and Princess Stephanie posing with some of the performers at the popular International Circus Festival.

Monaco and, at the same time, they make the outside world aware of the principality and its attractions.

Monaco's festivals are both religious and secular. Since more than 90 percent of the people are Catholic, religious celebrations like the Feast of Saint Dévote, as well as more universal celebrations such as Easter, can involve large numbers. The secular festivals, such as the Circus or the Fireworks Festival are likely to attract hundreds of additional visitors.

THE INTERNATIONAL CIRCUS FESTIVAL

Every January the best circus troupes in the world are invited to compete in this outstanding event, one of the most popular affairs of the year. A huge tent, with room for three rings and seating for more than 4,000 spectators, is set up in an area called the Espace Fontvieille.

More than 100 acts are entered in the competition, ranging from acrobats and trapeze troupes to lion tamers, elephant acts, and trained white tigers. Performers come from all parts of the world. Throughout an exciting week the international stars compete for prizes in several categories. The winners receive little statuettes called Clowns d'Ors (Golden Clowns), the circus world's equivalent of Hollywood's Academy Awards. The festival, which concludes with the Gala Awards Show, is one of the most thrilling circus shows in the world.

INTERNATIONAL FIREWORKS FESTIVAL

Another great competition is the annual International Fireworks Festival, held every summer since 1966. As the Mediterranean skies darken each night, fireworks specialists from around the world compete with

The beautiful fireworks at the International Fireworks Festival lighting up the night sky.

a colorful and noisy display of pyrotechnic skills. The show begins in July and continues through August.

The exciting display of fireworks can be watched from any number of venues, such as along the harbor, at outdoor cafés and terrace restaurants, the grounds of the palace, and along the ramparts of Fort Antoine. Every evening seems to offer a surprise or two, as specialists from Canada, China, the United States, Japan, Australia, and many parts of Europe vie for various prizes. The winning team returns in November for a display on the eve of Monaco's National Day, November 19.

A contingent of guards marching on the grounds of Monaco palace on National Day.

MONACO FESTIVAL OF THE SEA

Although Monaco Harbor is best known for its luxury yachts, the Fête de la Mer (Festival of the Sea) is quite different. Instead of big yachts with their own helicopter pads, the bay is filled every June with fishing boats, sailing vessels, and motorboats. The event celebrates Saint Peter, the patron saint of sailors.

The mixed regatta files through the port for blessings, followed by an array of activities. All classes of sailboats can take part in races, some of which are open to amateurs and others to professionals. There are also displays of different crafts and accessories.

Sailors can participate in different classes of regattas during the Festival of the Sea.

Monégasques proudly waving their principality's flags on National Day.

THE ROLE OF THE ROYAL FAMILY

National Day, which is also known as the Feast of the Prince, is held on November 19 each year, preceded by the award-winning fireworks display the evening before. National Day is a festive affair, with people in traditional Monégasque costumes taking part in a colorful parade to the palace. There is plenty of music, traditional folk dances, and a variety of foods. The prince makes a public appearance and spends part of the day greeting visitors.

The prince and other members of the royal family also play important parts in a number of annual events. In March they host the Rose Ball, a charity affair, followed in August by the Red Cross Gala Ball. Held in the Monaco Sporting Club the Red Cross Gala Ball is said to be the largest charity event in Europe. It brings together the social elite of the continent. More than 1,000 people pay $1,000 each to attend. The prince also hosts a picnic for the people of Monaco every June.

CALENDAR OF FESTIVALS AND HOLIDAYS

January 1	New Year's Day
January	International Circus Festival
	Feast of Saint Dévote
February and March	Carnival
March/April	Easter Sunday and Monday
May 1	May Day or Workers' Day
May	Feast of the Ascension
May/June	Pentecost/Whitsunday and Whitmonday
June	Feast of Saint John
	Monaco Festival of the Sea
July	Monte Carlo International Fireworks Festival
August	Feast of the Assumption
November 1	All Saints' Day
November 19	National Day (Fete Nationale)
December 8	Feast of the Immaculate Conception
December 25	Christmas

FOOD

LIKE PEOPLE IN OTHER COMMUNITIES along the Mediterranean coast, the people of Monaco love to eat. Whether they are enjoying food at home or in a restaurant, every meal is savored. Monaco has several outstanding restaurants, plus a surprising number with excellent food at moderate prices. For preparing meals at home, the open-air markets are outstanding for purchasing produce. Consumers know that the ingredients are fresh, and since the food is not prepackaged, they can buy only as much as they need.

The most important ingredients in the cooking of the region are olive oil, garlic, and local herbs—and freshness. The one constant demand of every chef and home cook is that every ingredient be as fresh as possible. The insistence on freshness is partly a product of history, because, until the age of modern transportation, local products were not transported very far. As a result, people learned to rely on the farm and fishing products of their area. Traditionally, for example, men on fishing boats from the Marseille region began preparing their famous bouillabaisse (fish stew) while the boat was sailing toward port. Today, a popular Monaco restaurant guarantees that fish, ordered for the midday meal, will have arrived in no less than two hours from the sea.

Above: **Fresh olives are readily available in Monaco and are often included in many dishes.**

Opposite: **The open air market in the Condamine quarter.**

MEALS AT HOME

Meal preparation is time-consuming because prepared foods are rarely used. But cooking is also simple, since recipes do not require complicated sauces or heavy seasoning. Many people eat their main meal at midday, but the requirements of most modern jobs make this increasingly difficult, so there is a growing trend toward evening dining. On holidays and other festive occasions people usually gather with friends and family for more elaborate meals. These meals can last two to three hours.

The people of Monaco usually shop every day or two, in order to have the freshest foods possible. A simple breakfast might require a trip to a neighborhood bakery, for example, in order to purchase a baguette (a long, pointed loaf of bread) that is still a little warm from the oven. To ensure its freshness the clerk does not put the loaf in a bag; instead a piece of paper is wrapped around the middle of the bread for carrying it. Freshly-squeezed orange juice and freshly brewed coffee would complete the meal, along with butter and jam and milk for the coffee. On some mornings the baguette might be replaced with croissants (buttery, crescent-shaped rolls), or *pain au chocolat* (puff pastry filled with chocolate).

Fresh produce is readily available in Monaco at markets like this one.

Shopping for the evening meal might be accomplished after work, with a pleasant stroll through the shaded stalls of an open-air market. Shoppers fill their baskets with fresh vegetables: tomatoes, cucumbers, onions, green beans, green peppers, and young potatoes. At home they cut these up, add ground fresh tuna, hard-boiled eggs, and anchovies, then top the ingredients with an olive oil–based dressing to make a *salade nicoise*, a creation from the next-door city of Nice. Dessert for this meal might be a local cantaloupe to serve with *navettes*, cookies flavored with anise and orange blossom.

FAVORITE FOODS

Many vegetable dishes are popular with Monégasques. They can be served with rice, pasta, or on its own. Some of the most popular ingredients are combined with a standard dish called ratatouille. This includes staples such as onions, eggplant (aubergine), zucchini, green peppers, and artichokes stewed together with tomatoes, garlic, and herbs.

A dish of ratatouille is made from a variety of vegetables.

Fresh vegetables can also be cut up and served raw as crudités with a dip such as anchovy paste mixed with garlic and olive oil. Stuffed vegetables are also popular, such as eggplant stuffed with ground or chopped meat, onions, and herbs, served in a tomato sauce.

Some soups are hearty enough to be self-contained meals. *Soupe de poisson* (fish soup), for instance, made with fresh fish, is served

A man selecting fresh produce at an open market in Monaco.

with crisp toast, a clove of garlic, and *rouille*, a spicy mayonnaise made with crushed chili peppers. *Soupe au pistou* is a thick, minestrone-like vegetable soup, served with *pistou*—a sauce made with garlic, basil, and olive oil—stirred into it.

Monégasques and other long-term Monaco residents are more likely to prepare seafood than meat. The variety of freshly caught fish is almost endless, but the most popular are probably sea bass, tuna, red snapper, mullet, anchovy, and cod. The most common meat is lamb, which is usually roasted with herbs. Beef is most popular in slow-cooked stews, called daubes, but is rarely seen as steaks or roasts. In the past wild game, such as rabbit, wild boar, and birds, was popular, but the decline of hunting has made game much less common in meals.

Fresh fruit is always popular, especially for use in desserts, and the region abounds in excellent varieties of fruit: oranges and lemons from Menton, Cavaillon melons, cherries from Luberon, and apricots, table grapes, and figs from various locations. The region is not famous for cheese, which is unusual since both France and Italy are known for their cheeses. Probably the best known is Banon goat cheese, a nutty goat cheese made in small disks that are individually wrapped in chestnut leaves and tied with raffia. In addition to fruit, popular desserts include custards, such as crème brulee, various fruit tarts, and all sorts of pastries. Ice cream is also common. The local favorite is a delicate chestnut ice cream.

DINING OUT

Monaco is famous for its four- and five-star restaurants, including two or three that are regarded as among the finest on the Mediterranean coast. As is the case with most modern cities, visitors can find just about all of the world's major cuisines. Monaco's restaurants tend to feature Italian and French recipes, and they rely heavily on seasonal foods, such as young asparagus in the spring, zucchinis and eggplant in summer, and figs and pumpkins in the fall. Pasta dishes are very popular—spaghetti, ravioli, and all sorts of small pastas. Some northern Italian recipes are based on rice. Even some of the great chefs use simple recipes, and most avoid the rich, creamy sauces of northern France.

A typical menu might include: hors d'oeuvres or some other starter, such as a soup or a paté; an entrée, most likely fish or an omelette; then a main course, consisting of lamb, beef, poultry, or game, along with a garni (vegetables with rice or potatoes). Next comes a green salad "to lighten the stomach," then cheese and dessert. Coffee, usually a strong espresso, is served by itself, rather than with the dessert.

The wine cellar at world-class restaurant, Louis XVI.

BOUILLABAISSE (FISH STEW)

The rich fish stew called bouillabaisse is probably the most popular dish in the entire Riviera region, including Monaco. No two versions of it are alike, and even the ingredients are likely to vary from one cook to the next. The name comes from the French *bouillir* (to boil) and *baisser* (to lower the heat). There are usually at least four different fresh fish cooked in a fish broth, or stock, but there can be as many as 10 or 12 different fish. Common fish used in Monaco's restaurants include shellfish, mullet, monkfish, snapper, conger eel, and the one fish that chefs say is most essential, scorpion fish. Usually the fish broth is served first over croutons, followed by the fish as a main course. (Bouillabaisse is also popular throughout Europe and North America.)

    2 onions
    olive oil
    chopped parsley
    clove of garlic
    2 pounds of fish, such as halibut or cod
    4 large tomatoes
    salt and pepper

Peel the onions under running water, then, on a cutting board, cut them into very thin slices. Chop the parsley and cut the garlic and tomatoes into small pieces.

In a deep skillet, brown the onions in olive oil. Add the parsley, garlic, and tomatoes. Simmer for 15 minutes. Cut the fish into bite-size pieces and add to the stew. Bring the mixture to a low boil and simmer for about 20 minutes. The fish should be cooked, but firm.

Ladle into soup bowls. Serve with French bread. Serves 4 to 6.

FLORENTINES (OR CHOCOLATE "LACE" COOKIES)

These delicious cookies are known both as Florentines and chocolate "lace" cookies, even though they have little or nothing to do with Florence and, although they are very thin, they are not really lace cookies. In any case they make a great dessert or snack. Florentines are popular throughout Europe.

½ cup whipping cream

3 tablespoons sugar

$\frac{1}{3}$ cup blanched and slivered almonds

¼ pound diced orange peel (available insupermarket baking departments)

¼ cup all-purpose flour

1 tablespoon unsalted shortening

4 ounces melted semisweet chocolate (or use prepared hocolate dip)

Preheat the oven to 350°F (177°C).

In a mixing bowl stir the whipping cream and sugar well. Stir in the almonds, orange peel, and flour.

Grease a cookie sheet with a thin layer of shortening and sprinkle a little flour on top. Drop the batter on the cookie sheet from a teaspoon. Keep well separated. Bake the cookies at 350° for 10 to 15 minutes, or until golden brown. Be very careful to check the cookies often because they burn easily.

Allow the cookies to cool, then spread the bottoms with the melted chocolate. Spread the chocolate with a spatula, or gently stick a fork into a cookie and dip it. Dry the cookies chocolate side up on wax paper.

Makes 30 thin, 3-inch wide cookies.

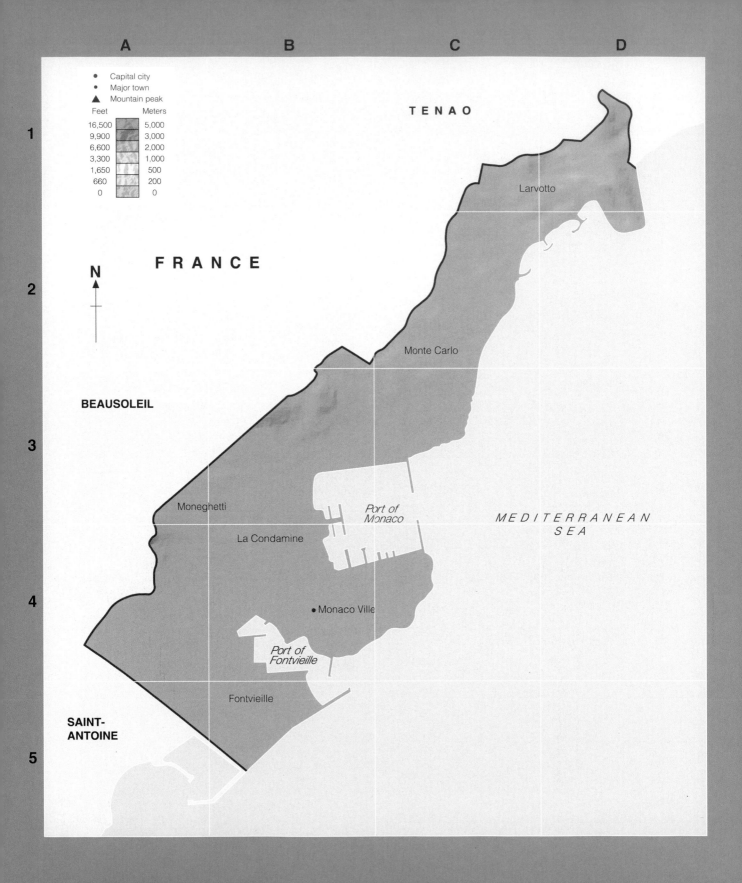

MAP OF MONACO

ECONOMIC MONACO

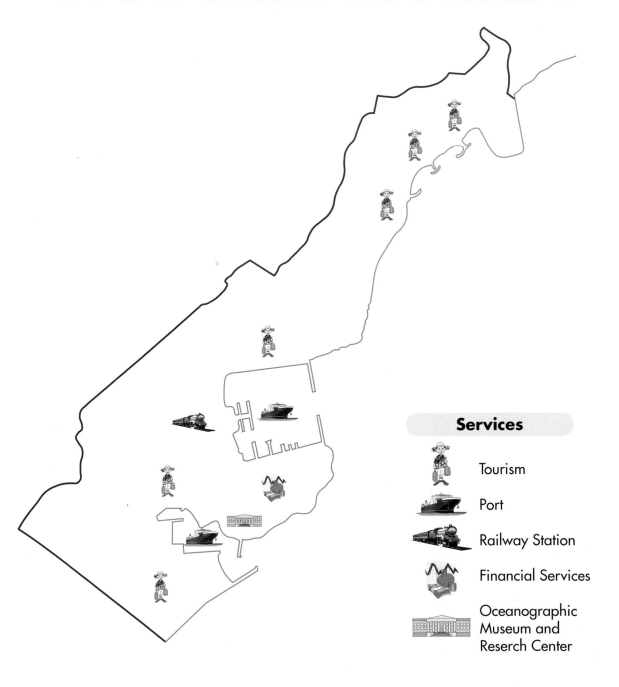

Services

Tourism

Port

Railway Station

Financial Services

Oceanographic Museum and Reserch Center

ABOUT THE ECONOMY

GROSS DOMESTIC PRODUCT (GDP)
$870 million U.S.

GDP GROWTH RATE
0.9 percent

GDP BY SECTOR
Tourism, light industry, construction

PER CAPITA INCOME
U.S.$27,000

WORKFORCE
43,000

UNEMPLOYMENT RATE
3 percent (2003)

POPULATION BELOW POVERTY LINE
0 percent

LAND AREA
0.76 square miles (1.97 sq km)

LAND USE
Agricultural land 0 percent

CURRENCY
1 USD = 0.792 euro (2007)

AGRICULTURAL PRODUCTS
None

NATURAL RESOURCES
None

INDUSTRIES
Tourism, construction, small-scale consumer products, banking

IMPORTS
511.86 million euros (2004)

EXPORTS
527.76 million euros (2004)

MAJOR TRADE PARTNERS
France, Italy, England, United States, Spain, Germany, Switzerland

CULTURAL MONACO

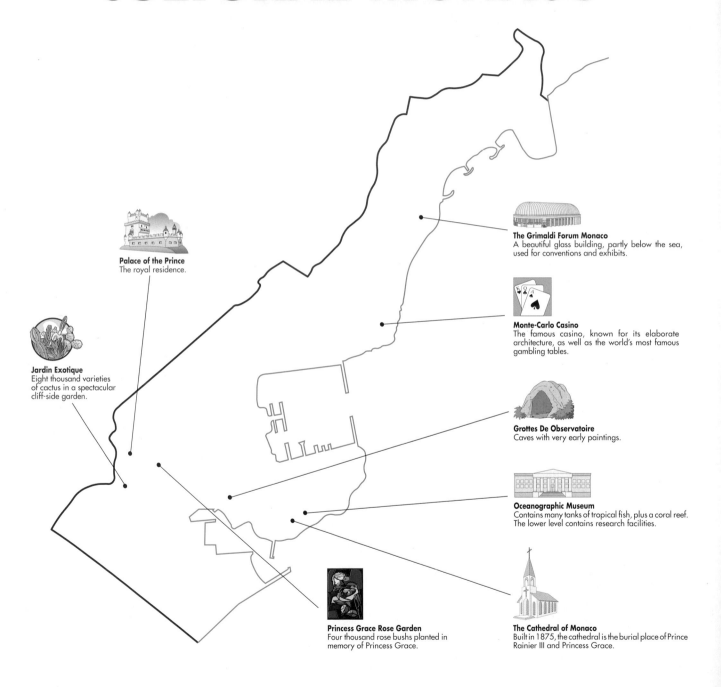

Palace of the Prince
The royal residence.

Jardin Exotique
Eight thousand varieties
of cactus in a spectacular
cliff-side garden.

The Grimaldi Forum Monaco
A beautiful glass building, partly below the sea,
used for conventions and exhibits.

Monte-Carlo Casino
The famous casino, known for its elaborate
architecture, as well as the world's most famous
gambling tables.

Grottes De Observatoire
Caves with very early paintings.

Oceanographic Museum
Contains many tanks of tropical fish, plus a coral reef.
The lower level contains research facilities.

Princess Grace Rose Garden
Four thousand rose bushs planted in
memory of Princess Grace.

The Cathedral of Monaco
Built in 1875, the cathedral is the burial place of Prince
Rainier III and Princess Grace.

ABOUT THE CULTURE

OFFICAL NAME
Principality of Monaco

NATIONAL FLAG
Two horizontal bands, with red on top, white on the bottom. The colors are from the Grimaldi coat of arms.

OTHER MAJOR AREAS
Fontvieille, Monte-Carlo, Moneghetti, La Condamine, Monaco-Ville

POPULATION
32,543 (July 2006 est.)

POPULATION DENSITY
32,543 per square mile (16,400 per square km)

ETHNIC GROUPS
French 32 percent; Monégasque 19 percent; Italian 20 percent; other 21 percent

LIFE EXPECTANCY
Male 75.7 years; female 83.6 years

RELIGIOUS GROUPS
Roman Catholic 90 percent; other 10 percent

OFFICIAL LANGUAGE
French

EDUCATION
Compulsory, ages 6 to 16

LITERACY RATE
99 percent

NATIONAL HOLIDAYS
Feast of Saint Dévote, January 27
Corpus Christi, June
Fete Nationale, November 19
Immaculate Conception, December 8

FAMOUS MONÉGASQUES
Léo Albert C. A. Ferré, poet, composer, singer (1916–93)
Louis Notari, writer (1879–1961)
Prince Albert I, explorer, ruler of Monaco (1848–1922)
Princess Grace, movie star (1929–82)
Prince Rainier III, ruler of Monaco (1923–2005)
Prince Albert II, ruler of Monaco (1958–)

TIME LINE

IN MONACO	IN THE WORLD
600 B.C. Greeks establish colony of Monoikos.	
120 B.C. Romans move in; Monaco is incorporated into the Roman Empire.	
A.D. 300–310 Romans persecute Christians; Saint Devote becomes a martyr.	
A.D. 400–500 Barbarian tribes from the east invade the region.	**A.D. 600** Height of Mayan civilization
	1000 The Chinese perfect gunpowder and begin to use it in warfare.
1215 Genoa establishes a fort on the Rock of Monaco.	
1297 François Grimaldi, disguised as a monk, seizes Monaco.	
	1530 Beginning of trans-Atlantic slave trade organized by the Portuguese in Africa.
1525 Monaco is placed under the protection of Spain.	**1558–1603** Reign of Elizabeth I of England
1612 Honoré II is the first Grimaldi to take the title of prince of Monaco.	**1620** Pilgrims sail the *Mayflower* to America.
	1776 U.S. Declaration of Independence
1793 French take control of Monaco during the French Revolution. Grimaldi family imprisoned.	**1789–99** The French Revolution
1815 Great powers of Europe place Monaco under the protection of the king of Sardinia.	
1861 Prince Charles III gives up Menton and Roquebrune to France in return for the guaranteed independence of Monaco.	**1861** The U.S. Civil War begins.

IN MONACO	IN THE WORLD
1863 Gambling begins at Monte-Carlo.	**1869** The Suez Canal is opened.
1911 Prince Albert I approves the first constitution.	**1914** World War I begins.
1929 First Formula One Grand Prix race is held.	**1939** World War II begins.
	1945 The United States drops atomic bombs on Hiroshima and Nagasaki.
1949 Prince Rainier III begins his 56-year reign.	**1949** The North Atlantic Treaty Organization (NATO) is formed.
1956 Rainier and Grace Kelly marry.	
1957 Oceanographer Jacques-Yves Cousteau becomes director of Oceanographic Museum.	**1966–69** The Chinese Cultural Revolution.
1982 Princess Grace dies after car crash.	**1986** Nuclear power disaster at Chernobyl in Ukraine
	1991 Break-up of the Soviet Union
1993 Monaco joins the United Nations.	**1997** Hong Kong is returned to China.
	2001 Terrorists crash planes in New York, Washington, D.C., and Pennsylvania.
2005 Prince Rainier III dies; Albert II becomes the ruling prince.	**2003** War in Iraq begins.

GLOSSARY

carabinieri
Guards.

Côte d'Azur
The Azure Coast. The coastal Mediterranean of southern France and Monaco.

croupiers
Casino dealers.

headland
A rocky point of land that pushes into the sea.

Kyoto Protocol
An international agreement to take vigorous steps to reduce the amount of greenhouse gases in the upper atmosphere. Monaco signed in 2005.

lifts
The word used in European countries for "elevators."

Les Petits Chanteurs de Monaco
The Little Singers of Monaco. The principality's famous boys' choir.

Monégasques
The native-born citizens of Monaco, making up about 16 percent of the population.

Palladienne
A Monégasque folk group of singers and dancers.

pétanque
A very popular team game, similar to lawn bowling.

principality
A small geographic area ruled by a prince.

proportional representation
A system of voting based on the percentage of votes received by each political party in the last election.

Saint Dévote
A Christian martyr who became the patron saint of Monaco.

FURTHER INFORMATION

BOOKS

Hewett, Michael. *Monaco Grand Prix: A photographic portrait of the world's most prestigious motor race.* Somertset, UK: Haynes Publishing, 2007.

Hintz, Martin. *Monaco* (Enchantment of the World Series). New York: Children's Press, a Division of Scholastic, 2004.

WEBSITES

CIA World Factbook (select Monaco from the country list). www.cia.gov/cia/publications/factbook/geos/Monaco

Official principality website. www.gouv.mc/devwww/wwwnews.nsf/Home

BIBLIOGRAPHY

Bell, Brian (editor). *French Riviera*. London, England: APA Publications, 2003.

Facaros, Dana and Michael Pauls. *South of France*. Guilford, CT: Cadogan, 2005.

Glatt, John. *The Royal House of Monaco*. New York: St. Martin's Press, 2002.

Noe, Barbara *A. Provence and the Cote d'Azur*. Washington, D.C.: National Geographic Society, Inc., 2003.

Williams, Roger. *Provence and the Cote d'Azur*. New York: DK Publishing Co., 2004

INDEX